"Dr. David Adams has written a book that comes from his heart, passion and personal expertise. The book is filled with words of wisdom, specific interventions that empower parents and stories from David's own parenting journey. For parents who are fostering and/or adopting, this book has been uniquely built to be your partner and guide as you navigate the emotional landscape of helping your child heal".

Allison Davis Maxon, LMFT, *Executive Director of the National Center on Adoption and Permanency*

"This book is a valuable resource for any parent who is trying to be the best parent they can be to their child with a challenging background. Dr David Adams brings together the powerful science of behavior and historically proven trauma-informed practices in a manner that is both informative and accessible".

Gabi Morgan, PhD, BCBA-D, *Assistant Professor of Applied Behavior Analysis, Cambridge College and Bay Path University*

"Dr. David Adams' book is both refreshing and insightful. Dr. Adams weaves his own personal stories as an adoptive parent as well as highlights pertinent information about trauma-informed parenting. This is a book that will inspire today's foster/adoptive parents. They will learn a great deal from this timely resource. I highly recommend this book to all who care for children in crisis".

John DeGarmo, *Founder and Director of Foster Care Institute*

"This riveting book provides a comprehensive guide for foster and adoptive parents. Drawing from his extensive clinical experience as a psychologist and behavior analyst, as well as his personal experience as a foster and adoptive parent, Dr. David Adams offers invaluable guidance. His approach emphasizes the importance of using connections to address dysregulated behaviors in children with a history of trauma. This book is an essential resource for parents and professionals working with traumatized children".

Kirsten M. Kosmerl, EdD, BCBA-D, BCASE, IBA, CTRT-E, CTRS-C, ACAS, ADHD-CE, LBS, LBA, *Educational and Behavior Consultant, certified trauma and resilience trainer*

"Dr. David Adams allowed us into his world with immersive details of his life as foster parent and a professional. He merges these two worlds to create a 'how to' guide for foster and adoptive parents. The book will also be an invaluable resource for professionals who work with foster parents as well. The 'Lessons Learned', section at the end of each chapter is a great quick reference guide. I recommend this book to anyone who wants an inside look into foster parenting".

Megan M Hamm, EdS, LPC-S, RPT- EMDR, *certified clinician, Parent-Child Relationship Expert*

"This is a must read for anyone caring for a child in out of home care. Dr. David Adams provides an honest portrayal of life with his children with their setbacks and successes. He shares how to handle the common behavioral issues for children in foster care along with the roots and meaning of these behaviors with a trauma-informed lens. This book will be an inspiration to all who are in the trenches with him. I cannot imagine a better guide for foster and adoptive parents to help their children grow and heal".

Martine Wehr, JD, *Foster and Kinship Care Education Program Director, Saddleback College, California*

"This inviting book moves the reader from theory to application with an accessible and encouraging text. If you have been trying to address challenging behaviors and are tired of cookie-cutter solutions, Dr. David Adams offers multiple strategies to meet the specific needs of your precious child and help you maintain connection".

Renae M. Dupuis, MDiv, *Founder of TraumaWise*

"Wow! Parents of all kinds will resonate with this insightful book, and caregivers of all kinds will appreciate and learn from reading Dr. Adams' vulnerable, revealing stories. Supporting therapists just might emerge more helpful as they approach future families who would benefit from an understanding of how trauma-informed view of challenges changed Dr. Adams' life and his children's behavior. This perspective could change your life and your parenting too".

Camille Kolu, PhD, BCBA-D, *Owner, of Cusp Emergence*

"This timely book outlines the realities of foster and adoptive parenting for children with trauma histories in a way that allows one to understand the why behind trauma-related behaviors. Foster and Adoptive parents and professionals will learn to be more mindful in their own responses, rather than to look at the behaviors of their children at face value. Parents that read this informative book will walk away with fresh hope and understanding as they are equipped with practical steps to be better parents for their children".

Issac Etter, *Adoptee and Founder*

"As an adoptive parent, I deeply resonate with his research-backed strategies and personal stories. Dr. Adams' amazing insights into trauma-informed parenting are both practical and compassionate, offering invaluable guidance for parents walking similar journeys. Dr. Adams does a great job of combining his expertise and own experience as an adoptive father, which makes this captivating book a powerful resource for anyone seeking hope in the depths of challenging parenting. I'm grateful for Dr. David Adams' work and highly encourage you to read it".

Max McGhee, *OrphanCare Pastor of Saddleback Church,*
TBRI® practitioner

Trauma-Informed Foster and Adoptive Parenting

Many foster and adoptive parents lose hope when they experience challenging and oppositional child behaviors. This book gives parents the tools and strategies to respond to these outbursts – particularly those that stem from a child's potentially traumatic history.

Drawing from behavioral research within an attachment and neurobiological framework, this transformative book offers practical guidance for foster and adoptive parents and professionals who seek to better understand and respond to a child with maladaptive behaviors. Based on his clinical expertise and his personal experience of being a foster and adoptive parent, Dr. David Adams highlights how trauma can impact children's brains and behaviors. With a comprehensive model for each behavior, this guide offers evidence-based strategies that parents can use to both avoid and respond to the most common behaviors including lying, disrespect, hoarding, and defiance. Complete with sample scripts, this book equips readers with the knowledge and tools to become more aware, responsive, and empathetic.

This invaluable guide is designed for parents and caregivers of foster and adopted children, as well as family therapists, psychologists, and other mental health professionals who work with these children and their families.

David Adams, Psy.D., LPCC, BCBA-D, is a proud adoptive parent, a licensed psychologist, and a licensed professional counselor. He is the Founding Director and President of New Life Psychology Group in Laguna Hills, a part-time professor at National University (ABA, School Psychology, Educational Counseling Department), and an expert trainer of Foster and Kinship Care Education (FKCE) at Saddleback College.

Trauma-Informed Foster and Adoptive Parenting

Methods for Managing Meltdowns, Mishaps, and Maladaptive Behaviors

DAVID ADAMS, PSY.D., LPCC, BCBA-D

Routledge
Taylor & Francis Group

NEW YORK AND LONDON

Designed cover image: Getty Images

First published 2026
by Routledge
605 Third Avenue, New York, NY 10158

and by Routledge
4 Park Square, Milton Park, Abingdon, Oxon, OX14 4RN

Routledge is an imprint of the Taylor & Francis Group, an informa business

© 2026 David Adams

ISBN: 978-1-032-98872-6 (hbk)
ISBN: 978-1-032-98871-9 (pbk)
ISBN: 978-1-003-60108-1 (ebk)

DOI: 10.4324/9781003601081

Typeset in Myriad Pro
by KnowledgeWorks Global Ltd.

Contents

Illustrations

Figures

Tables

Acknowledgments

Thank you to a charming and spunky five-year-old girl named, Uyen, who has lived in an orphanage in Danang, Vietnam, throughout her childhood years. I sponsored Uyen for the past 10 years through an agency called "Giving it Back to Kids" and made several visits to the orphanage to help train the staff. I went to Vietnam thinking I was the one who was going to help bring about change for them, but I was the one who really changed. When Uyen looked me in my eyes, wrapped her arms around me, and said, "Daddy", it stirred in my heart the passion to overcome apathy in my own life with a desire to be a father to the fatherless and a champion for the orphaned child (James 1:27). Without this experience, I may never have jumped blindly into the adventure of fostering and adopting.

My inspiration for writing this book comes from my experiences of fostering and adopting my two children (Andrew and Kayla). It's been a very fast and steep roller coaster ride of changing velocity for them with lots of loops, sharp turns, and detours along the way. Both are so resilient from their own trauma and have overcome so many obstacles and reminds me how to never give up and to bounce back from pain, rejection, and adversity. As they slowly put their trust in me by sharing the secrets of their vulnerable and vaulted hearts, their ability to take this risk involving this attachment dance changed their lives and radically altered the trajectory of our lives. As we have shared life together for the past eight years, they will be the first to point out that I am not always the best at reflecting the principles discussed in this book (especially in parenting those difficult teen years). In fact, I used to think I was a great dad until they reached those teen years when they started to be slightly more rebellious. Despite my limitations and inadequacies as a single parent, they know I will never stop trying and will never give up on them. Andrew and Kayla – I have not always been the best parent, but I love you more than you know!

There are many people who have shaped me as a parent over the years. I thank my parents for constantly believing in and supporting that crazy child of yours with a dream of adopting as a single parent. There have been numerous individuals and families who have helped support me by providing meals, prayer, and support over the years. My own support group through Saddleback Church has helped me navigate difficult and uncharted territories.

There are countless people who helped me in writing this book. There are too many to mention by name. Thank you to Kevin Miller for editing my book proposal to help make it more coherent. Thank you to the editing team at Routledge, including Julia Giordano, who believed in me and the need for this book. There were several experts and authors who provided me with content-based feedback: Allison Davis Maxon, Dr. John DeGarmo, Dr. Gabi Morgan, Martine Wehr, Renae Dupuis, Dr. Camille Kolu, Isaac Etter, Max McGhee, Megan Hamm, and Dr. Kristin Kosmerl.

Finally, I dedicate this book to all the foster parents, adoptive parents, kinship "carers", and professionals who invest in them! You are the unsung heroes across the globe who invest in the lives of hurting and traumatized children. I truly hope this book will inspire you to be a better parent or caretaker as it has done for me.

Introduction

I'm not sure what I expected when I became a foster/adoptive parent, but I certainly did not predict these types of verbal outbursts within the first few months of being a foster parent:

- "I hate you!"
- "You're not my real dad!"
- "If you loved me, you would send me back to my last foster home!"
- "I wish you never adopted me!"
- "F – you!"

Such outbursts were coming during the first year of providing a new home for my son (age nine) and daughter (age seven), including physical aggression, writing on walls, vulgar language, lying, hoarding, stealing, meltdowns, police involvement, and defiance. It wasn't long before I felt emotionally and physically abused and worn out by my own children. At times, I felt like I was a victim; however, in reality, I was simply a recipient of the effects of trauma in the lives of my own children who had spent most of their lives in foster care.

These outbursts didn't just happen at home. My children got kicked out of church. One child of mine even got kicked out of their social skills class (due to their extreme social behaviors). I dreaded every time I had to pick up my children in their afterschool program, as one of the staff would inevitably say, "Dr Adams, we need to talk …" And every time the school called me, my heart would sink. I doubted whether I was able to continue as a foster parent.

What eventually altered my self-perception was my ability to interpret my children's behaviors through a trauma-informed lens. This enabled me to develop strategies to take one day at a time, persevere through

DOI: 10.4324/9781003601081-1

the chaos around me, and not project my fears that my own child in foster care would end up in prison.

Despite their behaviors, my son and daughter were not bad kids! In fact, they were remarkably resilient children. They were funny, fun-loving, and compassionate. They were also desperate to be loved, but they also rebelled against it. Having been in foster care for more than half of their lives, during that time they had experienced so much hurt and rejection that they had developed a deep fear and distrust of others, especially authority and caregivers. Despite their behaviors, I realized they didn't hate me. They were desperate for someone to love and believe in them, but they were also afraid that the cycle of pain and rejection they had experienced would start all over again. They were learning to love, but fear held them back.

My children's behaviors were not only a response to their trauma, but they were also a form of communication to let me know they were wounded. Things were not okay for them. They did not know how to communicate this to me other than through their maladaptive behaviors. They were desperately trying to remain "in control" of their environment, no matter the cost. For them, this was a matter of survival. However, this survival instinct was also a strength that allowed them to cope with all kinds of hurts growing up. It would be easy for me to label my own children as manipulative children; however, when I was able to understand that they were simply using a strength-based survival tool, it helped to change my perspective. Over the long haul, my goal has been to try to help them learn new ways to cope and to teach them new skills to take control of their pain and hurts.

My goal as a trauma-informed foster parent is to help teach them to use more adaptive skills rather than using their maladaptive behaviors to survive!

Years later, my children are completely different. They have many ongoing struggles stemming from their traumatic history, challenges that they will likely have to battle for the rest of their lives. Chaos permeates our home, and we still have some major challenges. However, it all seems so different now. The reason? My increased capacity to grow as a loving, trauma-informed adoptive parent and see things through a trauma lens helped sustain me during the difficult times. Until I was able to grow through this, my disciplinary practices and responses to my children's maladaptive behaviors hindered rather than helped their recovery.

Although life can be messy at times, the joys of foster parenting and adoption far outweigh the challenges. My hope is that this book will provide a fresh wind of encouragement and understanding for you as you guide your children who are in foster care through their own battles to overcome the effects of trauma. In addition, I want to provide you with tips and tools to help you with the challenging behavioral problems you are facing right now.

Section I of this book explains trauma and trauma-informed care (TIC) and provides some tips on how to parent children who have experienced loss and trauma within the framework of the latest behavioral and neuroscientific research. Section II describes the principles of empowering, connecting, and correcting that serve as the heartbeat for Trust-Based Relationship Intervention (TBRI®). TBRI® focuses on attachment, neuroscience, and trauma. In Section III of this book, you will learn about the principles of behavior change supported by applied behavior analysis (ABA). ABA focuses on utilizing a positive approach to changing behavior by looking at the context of behavior within the contingencies in the environment. Although the roots of behaviorism tended to be more rigid, ABA has evolved over the years with a focus on positive behavior supports and TIC (Rajaraman *et al.*, 2022). Section IV takes a deep dive into specific behavioral problems associated with children who have been adopted or live in foster care.

The research from behavior analysis can help provide tools to parents so they can teach skills to their children. Section IV provides effective attachment-based behavioral strategies based upon the principles of behavior analysis for some of the most common behaviors that foster/adoptive parents observe, including homework battles, defiance, disrespect, lying, stealing, hoarding, and social media and gaming addiction.

My goal is to help inspire you to understand the "why" of your child's behavior. Once we understand the why, I hope to provide you with practical behavior management tools with "how" to address the maladaptive behaviors. Maladaptive behaviors are a term I use to reflect behaviors that serve a purpose or function (such as meltdowns, disrespect, hoarding, stealing, defiance, etc.), but they do not lead to more adaptive ways of coping and adjusting. When using the term "maladaptive behaviors", it is important to understand that your child has not learned more adaptive ways to express their needs, hurts, pain, or feelings. For example, an adaptive way to express frustration is to calmly express their hurt or to ask for extra help; on the other hand, maladaptive ways to express frustration would be to scream, to become defiant, to cuss, and to become verbally or physically aggressive to others.

Although this is not meant to be an exhaustive field manual for everything you may experience as a foster or adoptive parent, this book is designed to be a "Why"/"How to" manual for you. The practical tips, sample scripts, and suggestions in this book are drawn from the trenches with my own personal experience as a foster/adoptive parent and from what I've learned from other foster/adoptive parents and their children through my work as a clinical psychologist and behavior analyst. Hopefully, this book will encourage and inspire you to keep going even as chaos abounds. Although I am writing this book for foster/adoptive parents, I am confident this book will be an invaluable resource to professionals who work with foster/adoptive families as well.

Some readers may be tempted to skip straight to section four; however, if you do this, you'll miss out on all the foundational pieces of trauma and behavior research that lead up to Section IV. Therefore, you will gain the most from this book if you digest each chapter in progression rather than skip around.

A foundational principle of this book supported by revolutionary attachment-based neuroscience along with behavioral research is that a child's experiences can alter their behavior. In other words, the behaviors of your foster/adoptive child can change as their environment changes. As a foster parent, you have the wonderful opportunity to help change the experiences and story of your child. When you help change the environmental contingencies that have maintained your child's behavior, your child's behavior can and will change! This is truly revolutionary!

While parent-child attachment doesn't solve every problem, it can certainly help you and your child work through problems together. Your attachment serves as the backbone for you to be able to teach your child new skills to cope.

This book is about helping to create a new environment of safety, empathy, and support for your child so they can learn new skills. "At the center of therapeutic work with terrified children is helping them realize that they are repeating their early experiences and helping them find new ways of coping by developing new connections between their experiences, emotions, and physical reactions" (Van der Kolk, 2005, p. 401).

Throughout this book, I interchange the terms "foster parent" and "adoptive parent". I have had the wonderful privilege of being both a foster and adoptive parent. Although there are differences between foster and adoptive parents, the principles outlined in this book apply to both foster and adoptive parents. When referring to these terms, I am referring to any non-birth/first parent who is temporarily caring for a child. This can include relatives also known as kinship care including aunts, uncles, and older brothers/sisters who are temporarily raising and caring for a particular child. By foster care, I will also broaden the term to include non-birth/first parents who may have temporary guardianship of a child. Adopted parents are individuals who legally adopt a child and have permanent rights and responsibilities of parenthood. All in all, When I reference "foster parents", it likely will also apply to adopted parents and other caregivers as well. In addition, in this book, I have coined a term called "Trauma-Informed Foster Parent (TIFP)". I will use this term interchangeably to refer to both foster parents and adoptive parents. In addition, I will use the term "TIFP(ing)" to refer to "Trauma-Informed Foster Parenting."

It should be noted that I am careful in this book to avoid using the term "foster child". In reflecting upon their experiences, there are many adults and teens who did not like to be referred to as "foster child". In fact, some have referred to the term "foster child" as the "F" word. In my opinion, it is a label to be avoided as we must remember that the children in foster care are children first! Therefore, I choose to use the term "your child" or "your child in foster child" to help be more respectful about labeling a child that can be offensive to many!

Without a doubt, parenting my children has been the greatest experience of my life, but it has not come without heartache. This book will show you how to persevere through such heartaches and become a better champion for your child. There will, indeed, be times when you may feel like you have no idea on how to help your child. I have felt this way on a regular basis (usually when I am breathing); however, I am so thankful that I endured and pressed on with sacrificing for my child with the hope that things would be better in the future. The good news is that adoptees are resilient and healthy attachments between trauma-informed adoptive parents and their children will help facilitate healing from their emotions and maladaptive behaviors. This book will help provide you with tools on how to create an environment so that your foster/adoptive child will become more likely to bounce back from their hurts and hang-ups to become healthy and happy.

It is unfortunate that pearls only form when there is an irritant that gets in the way first. It may take a little longer than you imagined, but the most beautiful pearls take time and a lot of pressure to develop. It is about being able to persevere in the presence of those irritants.

There are several places in the book where I reference certain videos. I have shared some videos of me and my children on my website that correspond to various topics. When you see a statement that says, "See my website video", you can access my website at https://www.drdavidadams.com/trauma-informed-foster-and-adoptive-parenting.html. These short videos will hopefully inspire you and encourage you along your journey as well.

While writing this book, I realized that despite all my training, experience, and expertise, I have a long way to go as an adoptive parent. I still make mistakes, and I don't always do the best job of putting things back together. So, don't be discouraged if you fail to get things right the first time. We're all in this together!

References

Rajaraman, A., Austin, J.L., Gover, H.C., Cammileri, A.P., Donnelly, D.R., & Hanley, G.P. (2022). Toward Trauma-Informed Applications of Behavior Analysis. *J Appl Behav Anal*. 55 (1), 40–61.

Van der Kolk, B.A. (2005). Developmental Trauma Disorder: Toward a Rational Diagnosis for Children with Complex Trauma Histories. *Psychiat Annuls*, 35(5), 401–408.

Section I

Brief Overview of Trauma-Informed Foster Parenting

In the next few chapters, I will highlight through my personal story with my own children in taking a new placement. I will emphasize certain things that I found to be helpful in preparing my placement, including adjusting my expectations, developing a team around me, and actively working toward self-care as a habit (even before I received the placement of my kids). Hopefully, you will gain more knowledge about the practice of trauma-informed care so you can translate this knowledge into practical tools to help your foster/adoptive child. Finally, you will also learn more about the symptoms of trauma. By exploring the nuerobiology of trauma, you will gain a better understanding of how to respond to your own children.

DOI: 10.4324/9781003601081-2

Undertaking a New Adventure

1

Courage is not the same thing as fearlessness. Courage is trembling at every joint while stopping forward in your journey as a foster parent to the unknown abyss of uncertainty. It occurs when you take in a hurting child and center all your attention for the goal of helping to bring healing toward a little soul who is entrenched in pain, hurt, and rejection. As you step out of your comfort zone for a cause greater than yourself, you can find meaning and purpose in your life and in the life of your traumatized child.

Fostering and adopting a child with a trauma history requires courage and is one of the most exciting and noble adventures one can experience, but it certainly is not for everyone! I will share my experience in this book (both good and bad) to hopefully encourage you. If you are a seasoned adoptive parent who is experiencing hardships, there is hope you find in this book that you are not alone! These challenges you are experiencing now are very real. If you are a future foster/adoptive parent, I do not want to sugarcoat things in such a way that results in an unrealistic expectation of the challenges that you may experience as a foster parent. It is not easy! However, the good news is that there are things you can do to help prepare yourself for what is to come. The wonderful news is to see the results of your trauma-informed foster and adoptive parenting result in a greater connection with your child.

With excitement and anticipation and a bit of trepidation, I started the process of training to become a foster parent through my local county foster care program. I recall being a bit overconfident during the process. After all, as a child psychologist, I knew all about trauma and its effects on behavior. In addition, I recall thinking that if I just provided my kids with unconditional love, everything else would come together (like after a year or two). My idealistic mindset couldn't have been farther off

DOI: 10.4324/9781003601081-3

the mark. I thought the passage of time alone with my unconditional love would bring about healing. It is true that love can facilitate healing; however, my children's trauma festered as my children aged. While connection helps heal the brains of traumatized children, providing unconditional love to your children doesn't mean that everything will fall into place.

Foster/adoptive parents also need to understand how trauma affects the brains and behavior of children. This understanding will alter how they respond to their foster/adopted children, especially when such children are dysregulated. Dysregulation is a brain-related condition that is common for children with trauma histories where one's emotions, cognitions, physiology, or thoughts are heightened in such a way that impairs one's ability to stay calm and relaxed.

Some individuals and professionals may get in the habit of saying things like a child is having a "tantrum". That type of label seems to insinuate that there is something inherently wrong with the child or that the child simply lacks self-control. This type of thinking can cause us as parents or professionals to respond to the "tantrum" with strict disciplinary practices that run the risk of causing further harm to the child. When using the term "dysregulated", we come to understand that the problem is a problem of the environment in combination with the child's central nervous system. The child who is dysregulated may cry, yell, scream, or throw things in order to try to feel calm or regulated. These types of behaviors are also known as maladaptive. So, the behaviors are "maladaptive", and "dysregulation" is the type of internal turmoil that a child may experience with the inability to regulate their feelings.

Traditional disciplinary practices may not be effective for unattached and traumatized children. Parenting a child with trauma requires a different parenting approach. Therefore, when preparing for a placement, avoid my example. Rather than be naively optimistic or overconfident, be open to embrace a different parenting approach that embraces the principles of trauma-informed parenting.

When you say "yes" to your child with trauma, you're actually saying "yes" to sharing their heartache, pain, and broken dreams. It can take a huge emotional toil for foster and adoptive parents to embrace a traumatized child, but, oh, it is so

worth it as the sacrifices you make bring healing
for your child. It is amazing that attachment can
literally change the way your child's brain develops.
When your child begins to attach to you it is like
the sweet aroma that healing will eventually come.

———————

Fast-forward a few months into our placement, and my idealistic dreams were shattered. However, they also morphed into more realistic hopes and dreams for my children over the years, such as helping them build emotional and spiritual well-being, achieve a sense of purpose, and helping them keep themselves and others safe while aiming for connection even when they are dysregulated.

While training to be a foster parent, my teachers shared a few videos of kids who were waiting for a home. One of the videos featured two children named Andrew and Kayla (see video on my website: https://www.drdavidadams.com/trauma-informed-foster-and-adoptive-parenting.html). I contacted a social worker and let them know I was interested in Andrew and Kayla. In the process, I discovered that they were part of the Orange County Heart Gallery. This group consists of children who are considered "hard to place", usually due to their trauma background, age, and history of maladaptive behaviors. Well, I was up for a challenge (or so I thought). Little did I realize I was signing up for a job that I was totally unequipped for and being dropped straight into a war zone.

When I found out I was a "match" for Andrew and Kayla, I was bubbling over with excitement and fear. The social workers met with me to review the children's backgrounds and behavioral concerns. As a psychologist and behavior analyst, I have been trained not to get too scared when reading about a history of such behaviors, which are driven by the child's environment. While I thought I was well prepared, little did I realize the storm that was about to begin! Looking back, I realize, although I had the academic training, it still felt like I was dropped into a war zone with the expectation to figure out how to be a trauma-informed foster parent on my own. I know that I am not alone with this feeling as I have talked with hundreds of other foster/adoptive parents over the years.

As I was full of excitement as I drove Andrew and Kayla to their new home, they were grieving the loss of everything that was familiar to them and grappling with fears about their unknown destination. As I drove, Andrew and Kayla threw toys at me and told me to take them back. Kayla took out some lipstick and decided to share some of her artwork on the car seats. These initial behaviors were like a loudspeaker, broadcasting their fears. It was their fifth move to a new home, and their traumatic past led them to believe they were going to be hurt all over again.

My natural tendency is to overreact or handle the situation without a sense of understanding and patience. Their behavior reminded me of how hard it was for them to be ripped away from everything they knew and go to an unfamiliar home. In addition, the culture of my home would be very different from their previous experiences. For me to be able to support my kids and their needs, I would have to work toward building a connection with them. Furthermore, I needed to learn how to interpret and respond to their behaviors through a trauma-informed lens.

I reminded myself it was important for me to view their behaviors as normal reactions to abnormal situations.

As a practitioner, I realize that their disruptive behaviors, such as throwing their toys at me and drawing on the seats, were meeting a need, driven by fear. I could have said that Andrew and Kayla were manipulative kids, trying to disrupt the placement. If I had done that, it would have led me to engage in strict disciplinary practices that would be more harmful than helpful. However, my kids were not being manipulative. In reality, they were experiencing deep fear, and their brain's limbic system (the part that regulates fear) was fully activated.

An empathetic, trauma-informed parent has their radar locked onto their child's fear and understands how such fear drives behavior.

In the moment, it is much easier to see an "out-of-control" child. However, such a mindset will only lead to frustration. An empathetic, trauma-informed foster parent will embrace the child's pain and seek to understand their behaviors within the context of their environment.

When I brought my children to their new home and showed them around the house, Andrew and Kayla were filled with a mixture of excitement, fear, grief, and anger. As I was showing Andrew his room, the first thing Kayla did was to run to the refrigerator to see what goodies were inside. She was excited to see ice cream in the freezer (see the video on my website of my kids exploring their new home for the first time (https://www.drdavidadams.com/trauma-informed-foster-and-adoptive-parenting.html)).

The first two weeks were a bit of a Disneyland experience. I was able to take two weeks off from work so I could spend all my time with Andrew and Kayla. Each day, we would do fun activities, such as going to a petting zoo or the park as we explored new places. It was so neat to see the expressions on the kids' faces. I did my best to bond with them. We also spent a lot of time in the pool. We all loved the pool, and I found it was a great way to get the kids to share a fun experience while also getting more comfortable with me. I had the opportunity to throw them into the air, teach Kayla how to swim, and watch them splash each other. I'm so thankful for our pool experiences. It was probably one of the greatest ways for me to bond with my kids.

Expect Some Troubles Along the Way

When your child first arrives at your foster home, you may experience a "honeymoon" of sorts for a few weeks, but it is important to anticipate that there will be some bumps and regression along this marathon journey. In fact, regression is normal. Typically, one does not make progress without regression and detours. The greater the regression, the greater the nurture! It is important when regression does occur to focus on connection and repairing what is ruptured. Normally, I encourage foster/adoptive parents to be optimistic, but it is also important to be realistic in knowing that it will be a huge adjustment for your child. There are many fears that your child likely embraces, so your role during the early parts of a placement is to promote safety and to build rapport and connect as much as possible with your child. Your child may not be ready to connect with you, so it is important to realize that you may see behaviors that push you away. Their actions may tell you, "I cannot trust you. I may get hurt". As you can interpret their behaviors as a form of communication to let you know this process is very scary for them, it will help you be more patient and understanding.

It is rare for a child in foster care to be grateful and open their arms to your love at the beginning of placements. Their brains are telling them to be on guard and to be cautious as a self-protective mechanism. Their experiences from their past are still etched in their thoughts, their feelings, and their neurology! My kids were telling me "Send us back" from day one. When/if this does occur, I suggest that you really focus on attempting to meet the needs of your child. Showing empathy, support, and letting your child know that you are going to try to support them in their pain the best you know how.

It is common for foster/adoptive parents to consider wanting to throw in the towel when regression and problems come. Many parents have thoughts like:

- Am I really suited for this?
- Am I a bad parent? How come I can't seem to help my child in foster care?
- Will my child ever trust me?
- My child is triggering me!

It is normal to have these types of thoughts at times. If you do, I strongly encourage you to get support from others and try to take one day at a time, rather than projecting your fears of tomorrow upon your experience today. The key is to expect that this will occur and commit before it happens that you will do your best to stay patient and continue the course.

When your child who is adopted slowly opens the secrets of their vaulted heart to you and begins to trust you, it will make the experience of hearing their affectionate words and behaviors something you will never forget! Your patience is worth the wait!

Building a Team Around You

I have always been an independent person, so I was unaccustomed to asking for help. However, this was one thing that I had to learn how to do. Luckily, I had a great team around me. I received donations of toys and clothes from my friends, and a group of people from my church helped me paint Andrew and Kayla's rooms and get them set up. They say it takes a village to raise a child, and this is so true. As a single parent, I needed the support of my friends and family. And over time, I realized that others wanted to help and support me. I just needed to learn how to ask for it. This was not always easy, but over time, I got better at it (out of necessity). There is no shame in realizing and embracing your interdependence with others. In fact, your child will need many champions who will advocate and fight for them. Champions who can provide you with respite and can connect with your child and lovingly engage them as well. I couldn't have done it without the support of my family and friends (see the video on my website: https://www.drdavidadams.com/trauma-informed-foster-and-adoptive-parenting.html).

When preparing your life and home for a hurt or traumatized child, you need to gather a village around you. Don't be afraid to ask for help. You will need it. You may want to intentionally plan respite breaks if possible. Most families with difficult children need healthy breaks away from their kids. If you are unable to do an overnight break, at least have some babysitters and/or respite care who are ready to jump in at short notice to support you.

I currently meet with a support group of other foster/adopted parents once a week. I have found that well-intentioned parents will often give me advice with things like, "you just need to discipline your kids more" or "you should just give that boy a spanking!" Other parents without foster/adoptive kids cannot possibly understand the challenges of building attachment with a child who is pushing you away. For this reason, I have gained an incredible amount of support and encouragement from the foster care/adoption support group that I facilitate. I am one of the facilitators of the group, but I gain so much from the other foster care/adoptive parents who provide me with empathy and understanding of the challenges that I face on a regular basis with my kids. It is a group where we all support each other, but at the same time receive support and encouragement. I could not imagine doing this without having a support team around me. If you do not have a group of friends who will drop the hat for you or your kids, please try to invest in developing one as soon as possible.

Begin With Self-Care in Mind to Help Overcome Compassion Fatigue

Foster parents are expected to put their child's needs over their own needs. The fact that you are a foster parent probably means that you have made dozens of sacrifices for your child. At times, you may get to a point where you are literally running out of your reserves without getting adequate sleep. You may have given up certain hobbies, certain social interactions, and certain freedoms by investing in the life of a hurting child. In fact, the more empathy that you provide for your child, the greater the opportunity that you may become distressed yourself.

Compassion fatigue has been defined as the negative cost of caring for others (Figley, 1995, p. 7). This term was first coined by Carla Joinson, a nurse, who discovered that nurses often develop symptoms of fatigue and lack of motivation due to their repeated care for patients in emergency rooms (Joinson, 1992, pp. 118–120). In a sense, it is possible for your child's suffering to result in your suffering. This is what compassion fatigue is all about.

Compassion fatigue is the unfortunate blend of caregiver traumatization and burnout. This is also referred to as secondary trauma. There are emotional and behavioral symptoms and physical symptoms of compassion fatigue. Some of the emotional and behavioral symptoms of compassion fatigue include the following: inability to relax, sleeping issues, anxiety, feelings of helplessness, reduced ability to empathize, restlessness, anhedonia (loss of pleasure), decreased interest in activities, social withdrawal from others, and engaging in addictive behaviors. Difficulties with sleeping, gastrointestinal issues, and headaches are common physical symptoms of compassion fatigue. It can lead to clinical forms of depression as well. It is often those parents who are so others-focused and quite sensitive and proactive to the needs of others as they invest all their attention in their child to the exclusion of their own needs.

"Blocked Care" is a term used in the foster care/adoptive world to reflect the type of compassion fatigue that we often experience. Blocked care is a type of compassion fatigue that reflects this type of internal barrier that occurs in a foster/adoptive parent due to the stresses related to parenting a child with a trauma history. In short, blocked care is a "self-protective mechanism in the nervous system activated by excessive stress. This suppresses the higher brain functions needed for caregiving, causing your nervous system to develop a defensive stance toward your child. Your heart seems to have left the relationship" (Qualls & Corkum, 2023, p. XV).

Over the years, I have worked with many foster/adoptive parents who admit that they simply do not like the child under their care. This can be hard for some who have never experienced "blocked care" or compassion fatigue to imagine, but these kinds of temporary feelings can be a common occurrence for parents who are raising children with a history of trauma with attachment-based behavioral outbursts. Very well-intentioned parents can have temporary seasons with uncomfortable feelings of disgust for their own children in part due to issues associated with blocked care. Guilt and shame can build up for parents who are raising children with trauma histories. All in all, if you are struggling with these types of feelings as a foster/adoptive parent, you are not alone. You are not crazy, and there is hope that things can and will change!

It is also important to understand the neurobiology of blocked care as a biological process of the effects of stress in your life from the difficult task of caring for a youth with so much pain in their life. Hopefully, as you recognize that compassion fatigue/blocked care is a neurobiological process in your body, it will help to reduce shame and guilt that you may experience as a foster/adoptive parent.

It is important to be aware of the symptoms of compassion fatigue so you will be able to more quickly intervene and respond to the effects of secondary trauma. By definition, a trauma-informed foster parent is trained to tap into the needs and symptoms of their child's trauma. They are extra sensitive to the trauma symptoms of their child. This extra sensitivity (if left unchecked) can easily be absorbed into secondary trauma for the caregiver (Teculeasa *et al.*, 2023, p. 309). There are a few characteristics that are common for foster/adoptive parents resulting in a greater susceptibility for compassion fatigue, such as lack of support, poor work-life balance, and the lack of personal self-care.

Self-care is the key to helping overcome the effects of compassion fatigue and blocked care. Self-care can be challenging for many foster/adoptive parents. Whether you are a seasoned adoptive parent or just beginning as a foster parent, I implore you to begin with self-care in mind! The question is not if you are going to burn out, but the better question is when are you going to burn out? I have yet to meet a foster or adoptive parent who has not at one point experienced mental and physical exhaustion from their care for their child under their care. It can be quite distressing having to live with a child with significant behavioral and emotional concerns, so unfortunately, this results in the caretaker feeling like they are living with constant stress in their life.

There are several behavioral strategies that you can do to help prevent compassion fatigue and/or blocked care from creeping in the front door. First, no matter how strong and dedicated you are, there is absolutely no way you can do it all by yourself! It is just not possible.

There are several things you can do to avoid compassion fatigue and the effects of blocked care in your life.

Depend upon others to help you care for your children

Develop healthy friendships and make sure that you do not completely isolate yourself or your family. As mentioned before, gather a team of friends, babysitters, next-door neighbors, and relatives who are a phone call away and are willing to drop everything to help support you in a time of crisis.

Don't lose your hobby and interests

It is important to find an outlet to release stress. Whether it is taking a jog, going to get a massage, or watching a movie, do it and then repeat! If you are married, never lose sight of the value of going on dates (at least once a month!). Yes, that is so easy for me to say as a single parent, but I said it ☺. Whether you are single or married, you can find time to be by yourself. Schedule respite and repeat! There have been many times that I have retreated to the bathroom to pretend to use the bathroom to try to get a bit of alone time, but even that did not always work as my kids would bang on the bathroom door!

Practice gratitude!

Researchers show that being grateful is one of the healthiest emotions to experience on a regular basis. It will help you with perspective when everything else seems like it is falling apart

Learn to practice boundaries

I have met many foster parents who struggle with setting boundaries. After all, we are so others-focused that it can be hard for us to say "No" at times. Learn to say "No" more often. Also, advocate for your own needs, even when others may not understand or agree.

Seek therapy

A therapist can help you process your feelings and encourage you to develop some healthy strategies to develop emotional wholeness again.

Practice self-care

Self-care is one of the best strategies to practice on a regular basis to avoid compassion fatigue. This includes making sure you eat healthy meals and have a proper diet. In addition, regular exercise will help to make sure that you have the physical stamina needed to endure the hardships that come with fostering or adopting a child with special needs.

Develop a healthy work-life balance

If you work outside the home, be sure to keep boundaries and keep work at work if possible.

Maintain a consistent sleep routine

I know, many of you may be thinking…yeah, right! Wish I could! It may be hard, but try to keep it a priority when possible.

Acknowledge your own loss

Taking a new child into your home is one of the most exciting adventures you can do in life! However, there is loss associated with any great change. Qualls and Corkum (2023) identified some of these losses as: loss of family and culture, loss in your marriage relationship, loss of normalcy, loss of belonging, loss of safety, loss of friends or extended family, and loss of privacy.

Take time to grieve your own hurts and loss

You will experience many hardships as a parent of a child with a history of trauma. There may be times when you may feel like giving up. Take time to acknowledge and grieve your hurts. Also, understand that our feelings can change quickly. Don't lose sight of the growth of your child, and understand it takes time to build attachment.

If you do develop compassion fatigue, it is important to normalize the experience. Guilt only contributes more to compassion fatigue. It is not your fault! In fact, the fact that you have compassion fatigue means that you have a heart – a heart that cares for others.

Also, I am very strategic about talking about self-care at the beginning of this book. Don't wait until you are already feeling tired to engage in self-care. Whether you are preparing for a new placement or are a seasoned foster/adoptive parent, develop an unwavering commitment to self-care without compromise

---

Lessons Learned

1. Take time off from work to build rapport and adjust.
2. Understand the role of fear and how this can impact your child's behavior.
3. Try not to take things personal when your child may say hurtful things to you or engages in certain distancing behaviors. This is all normal for the hurting and scared child.
4. Build memories together by creating rituals and traditions, being fully present with your child, and captivating upon opportunities to share quality 1 × 1 time with each other.
5. Introduce change slowly.
6. Build a village of support around you, and find people you trust who can provide babysitting and respite opportunities for you.
7. Make sure you get plenty of sleep/rest. You may not have "rest" on your to-do list, but put it on there now. Rest needs to be a priority. Be creative in finding time for yourself. As a single parent, the one place I have learned I can get some privacy is the bathroom. I have had some extended stays there!
8. Exercise. Hard exercise releases serotonin in your body, and serotonin is a neurotransmitter that can help put you in a positive mood.
9. Get a babysitter and go on a date with your partner or hang out with a friend.
10. Practice mindfulness. Be present in the moment. Enjoy the sunset. Experience the awe of a snail moving or the sound of a bird chirping.
11. Spend time with a hobby/interest. Your hobbies can be a great way to help replenish your tank.
12. Don't be afraid to ask for help.

    • Asking for help is a sign of strength, not weakness. There is no shame in seeking therapy for yourself.

References

Figley, C.R. (Ed.). (1995). *Compassion Fatigue: Coping with Secondary Traumatic Stress Disorder in Those Who Treat the Traumatized*. Brunner/Mazel.

Joinson, C. (1992). Coping with Compassion Fatigue. *Nursing*. 22 (4), 118–120.

Qualls, L.C., & Corkum, C. (2023). *Reclaim Compassion: The Adoptive Parents' Guide to Overcoming Blocked Care with Neuroscience and Faith*. Adoption Wise Press.

Teculeasa, F., Golu, F., & Gorbanescu, A. (2023). What Mediates the Link Between Foster Parents' Sensitivity Toward Child Posttraumatic Stress Symptoms and Job Satisfaction? The Role of Compassion Fatigue and Foster Parent-Child Relationship. *J Child Adolesc Trauma*. 16 (20), 209–320.

Unique Symptoms Associated with Trauma

2

Trauma is the result of an overwhelming sense of inescapable threat and fear; on the other hand, healing is the result of feeling safe, secured, empowered, and connected!

This chapter may be distressing for you. Nothing stirs up more discomfort than reflecting about the hurts, rejection, and trauma our kiddos have had to endure. However, it is necessary for us to be aware of how trauma affects the children under our care. This knowledge and understanding will also help facilitate you to have discussions with your child if/when they feel comfortable talking to you about how their history and experiences impact them today as well. Despite being such a difficult topic to explore, there is hope that stable and nurturing relationships can help facilitate healing.

The kids under your care likely have experienced horrific, toxic environments. Any disruption of a placement can be a traumatic experience for a child, even when they are removed from a harmful environment. It should not be taken lightly how excruciating it must be to be ripped apart from their parents, often by an unfamiliar adult or police officer. This kind of loss usually does not just go away on its' own. For many children in foster placements, their disruptions and trauma occurred at a young age when their neurological development is still in the process. These types of early experiences can significantly impact their development and their functioning throughout their life. Your child may be too young to remember being separated from their parents, but research proves that this kind of traumatic experience certainly impacts the neural circuitry and functioning of their brain (Cross *et al.*, 2017, p. 111).

The impact of exposure to domestic violence, neglect, physical abuse, sexual abuse, emotional abuse, and multiple changes in caretakers can affect the developmental trajectory of your child. Research shows

DOI: 10.4324/9781003601081-4

that these kinds of exposures have the potential to stunt the physical, social, emotional, and cognitive development of your child. This impact of neglect and abuse can limit the connections of the brain that are needed for the development of language. Indeed, trauma impacts the brain development of our children (American Academy of Pediatrics, 2020). We may not be able to observe how these experiences impact their brain without special equipment, but we certainly can observe how these experiences impact their daily behaviors. All aspects of a child's life and development (cognitive, emotional, physical, social, and behavioral) can be altered by trauma. This chapter highlights many of the symptoms and behavioral patterns that can be shaped by the effects of childhood trauma.

As foster or adoptive parents, it is important to be cognizant of the trauma symptoms of your foster/adoptive child. As you can better understand the toxic effects of trauma on the brains and behaviors of your child, you will be better equipped to respond to the challenges you will encounter. Trauma-informed foster/adoptve parents seek to adjust their parenting approach to address these symptoms. However, one cannot do this unless they are aware of the behaviors of their adopted child that stem from their trauma history. On the other hand, if one does not interpret their child's behavior in the context of their trauma, foster parents will run the risk of using an ineffective and even a harmful parenting approach that can possibly retraumatize their child. Unfortunately, a well-intentioned foster or adoptive parent may unintentionally retraumatize their child by their reactions when a child's trauma symptoms surface.

For example, let's say your child becomes fearful of a situation and lashes out with aggression or verbal disrespect to you. If you were to seek to punish the child or show signs of disapproval of their behavior, you are pushing your child away from you and creating distance in your relationship. They really need to see you as a safe person, and your response is to push them away in disgust. Your child desperately needs to trust you. When the trust of a child is violated through a traumatic event or experience, it can lead to life-long problems without intervention. Therefore, trauma-informed foster parents are constantly aware of the symptoms and effects of trauma for their child, so they do not inadvertently retraumatize their own child.

Trauma can be very complex to define as what is traumatic can greatly vary on the situation and the person. One reason it is difficult to define is that trauma is not just defined by the EVENT, but it is defined by the

EVENTS	EXPERIENCE	EFFECTS
Life threatening or extremely frightening events	A child's experience is the factor that determines whether or not it is traumatic	Can include physical, social, emotional, or spiritual consequences

Figure 2.1 Symptoms of Trauma

Terms in the table were outlned by SAMHSA (2014).

EXPERIENCE and EFFECT that it has on the survivor (SAMHSA, 2014). The EVENTS of childhood trauma include circumstances that can be life-threatening or an extremely frightening experience that may include neglect, physical abuse, sexual abuse, emotional abuse, domestic violence, etc. The EXPERIENCE of trauma may differ from child to child as what is traumatic for one child may not be traumatic for another. It is also true that a child may go through a horrific EXPERIENCE and yet have little EFFECT due to various factors; therefore, a child's EXPERIENCE of the EVENT is what is determined to be traumatic. These events may be events that your child either experienced or witnessed. The EFFECTS of the trauma can include physical, social, emotional, or spiritual consequences.

Trauma experiences in a young child can result in imprints in their brain and result in significant behavioral problems. Trauma also can affect the development of the child (including the development of their brain). Childhood trauma can affect emotional, cognitive, and social development. Obviously, this trauma can drastically impact your child's ability to trust and attach to you. We may think that if you just provide your child with enough love, your child will adjust. However, the developmental changes that occur need more than just love to heal. The good news is that the brain is malleable. It changes. We know that trauma impacts the brain, but we also know that one's behaviors can change the brain as well (Geng et al., 2021).

Indeed, trauma can result in a child learning poor ways to cope with stress. In fact, when attachment between parent and child is disrupted, it can lead to emotional instability and challenges in one's ability to regulate their emotional state. Research shows that a stable parent-child attachment will result in a child who can be more easily comforted and tends to bounce back from disappointment (Siegel, 1999). The key is that the environment of a child can drastically impact the temperament and skills that your child can utilize to cope with adversity. However, the research in neuroplasticity of the brain is great news as we seek to change the story of our kids! This research can give us hope that there is the possibility for the brain (and behaviors) of your child to change! No matter your child's age, you can help your child learn new strategies to respond to stress and fear, which will in return aid in your child's emotional, behavioral, and neurobiological recovery.

It is important to understand how trauma impacts the brain and how the brain impacts the behavior. This chapter four will provide an overview of how trauma affects behavior, but has a lot more detailed and technical information for you to better understand how trauma impacts the brain and health outcomes. Chapter four is a bit technical with neuroscience jargon, so don't be alarmed if it is a bit hard to grasp all the information in it.

There are three main types of traumas. Acute trauma consists of a frightening experience that is more time-limited. These types of events are usually one-time events such as witnessing domestic violence on a specific date. Acute trauma can lead to chronic trauma when there is no resolution. Chronic trauma is a term used to refer to repetitive, ongoing traumatic events such as a child who has been repeatedly hit by their stepfather on many occasions. Complex trauma is a type of chronic trauma. However, it is distinguished from complex trauma in that involves trauma of a young child (usually under the age of 5) and involves the child's primary caretakers or parents.

When looking at the maladaptive behaviors of a child who has been a survivor of trauma, Dr. Bruce Perry (a pioneer of childhood trauma) encourages us to shift our thinking from asking "What is wrong with this child?" to "What has happened to this child?" (Perry & Winfrey, 2021). It is important to understand that a child's behaviors are a product of his/her environment. The symptoms of childhood trauma can be so pervasive that it can affect a child's health, behaviors, and pathology.

As a foster/adoptive parent, it is important to understand how your child's trauma affects their brain and behavior. We know that trauma is defined by both the event and the emotional response (or behavior) of a child. There is a wide range of symptoms and behaviors of childhood trauma that can be challenging for foster and adoptive parents. This can include symptoms of emotional dysregulation, attention problems, sleeping issues, physical problems, and other behavioral problems. The

Diagnostic and Statistical Manual for Mental Health Disorders (DSM-5) outlines various symptoms of posttraumatic stress disorder (PTSD). It outlines how trauma can affect the cognitions, mood, and emotional or physical reactivity of your child (APA, 2013). These maladaptive behaviors may seem extreme, but they are NORMAL responses to the effects of trauma (Evans & Coccoma, 2014). There is a wide range of behavioral problems you may observe in your foster/adoptive child. Your foster/adoptive child may experience some of these, all of these, or other behaviors that can be related to their trauma. By no means, is this an exhaustive list, but this list of symptoms and behaviors that can be associated with childhood trauma; however, one does not have to have all these symptoms to be diagnosed with PTSD.

Table 2.1 Trauma Symptoms

Thinking Processes and Mood	Intrusive Symptoms	Avoidant Symptoms	Arousal and Reactivity Symptoms
Difficulty experiencing positive affect	Unwanted upsetting memories	Avoiding triggers	Physical reactivity or emotional distress after exposure to trauma reminders
Decreased interest in activities	Nightmares	Feeling isolated	Hypervigilance
Negative affect	Flashbacks	Inability to recall key features of the trauma	Heightened startle reaction
Exaggerated self-blame			Risky or destructive behaviors
Negative thoughts and assumptions about oneself, the world, and others			Difficulty Concentrating
			Irritability or aggression
			Difficulty sleeping
			Depersonalization
			Derealization

Trauma Symptoms Outlined by APA (2013)

Thinking Processes and Mood

Symptoms of trauma can be grouped into one of four clusters of symptoms. One group of symptoms related to trauma includes changes in a child's thinking processes and mood. This includes symptoms of exaggerated self-blame, depression, difficulty experiencing positive affect, negative affect, and a decreased interest in activities (APA, 2013).

It also includes the negative assumptions that your child may have regarding the world, themselves, and others. Dr. Aaron Beck referred to this reality as the "cognitive triad" (Beck *et al.*, 1987). Unresolved and unaddressed trauma will rob our children of the ability to interact with others in healthy ways, and it will result in a negative belief system and ideas about the world, their future, and their own self views, also known as thier "internal working model" (Bowlby, 1969/1982).

Negative assumptions of the world, negative assumptions of self, and negative assumptions of the future were from SAMHSA (2014).

Negative assumptions of the world

It is possible that your child will have negative assumptions about the world or self. For example, many traumatized children like to be in control of their environment as it becomes hard for them to trust adults in their lives. They may also have a belief system that the world is not safe, so they constantly must be on guard for threats. Your child's trauma may make it difficult for your child to attach to you due to their experiences and their belief system that others cannot be trusted. It can be easy to see how your child would have fears of being abandoned once again! Your child may have such thoughts:

- The world is not safe
- My neighborhood is dangerous
- My home is a scary place
- No one can be trusted
- I must take care of myself (as I can't trust you!)
- I must be in control of everything and at all costs

If you wonder why your child likes to be in control all the time, it may have to do with their unfortunate and traumatic experiences that other people cannot be trusted.

Negative assumptions of self

Others may have inaccurate assumptions about themselves as they may feel different or damaged. My daughter came to me when she was in the second grade and could not read. She constantly would tell me and other people that she was "stupid". When I tried to remind her that this was not true, she would respond, "No, it is. Everyone knows this!" I tried to help her see how she labels herself as stupid to other people, and that it is important for her to see her own strengths. However, her belief system that she was stupid was very ingrained in her mind. Many children who are survivors of childhood trauma will have such kind of thoughts:

- I am a bad kid
- I can't do things right
- I am different from others
- I am defective
- I do not have any strengths

Negative assumptions about my future

Childhood trauma also can affect one's beliefs about their future and feel hopeless that things will change for the better. These assumptions can carry them into adulthood, especially if they are not actively seeking recovery. Your child may have some a mindset with such thoughts:

- It is hopeless
- Things will never change
- Why even try?
- It is useless!

If your child has a "fixed mindset" such as some of the beliefs outlined above, you may consider looking at curriculum that focuses on the "growth mindset". The term "growth mindset" was developed by Carol Dweck. The idea is that a person can learn to improve their abilities and talents by developing a positive mindset and being willing to work hard and embrace challenges. This is often taught in educational systems

Views about the world
"The world is a dangerous place"
"People cannot be trusted"
"Life is unpredictable"

Views about self   Views about the future
"I am incompetent"   "Things will never be the same"
"I should've reacted differently"   "What is the point? I will
"It is too much for me to handle"   never get over this"
"I feel damaged"   "It is hopeless"

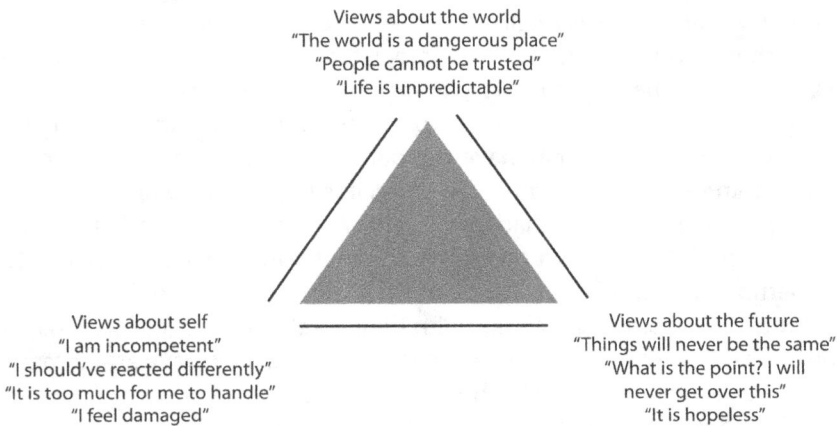

Figure 2.2 Cognitive Triad of Stress
ADAPTED from SAMHSA (2014).

and helps teach children to embrace challenges and to be willing to try hard things (Dweck, 2007).

Intrusive Symptoms

A second cluster of symptoms related to trauma are intrusive symptoms. This includes unwanted and reoccurring thoughts about the traumatic event. It also includes symptoms of flashbacks and nightmares (APA, 2013). Intrusive symptoms can be difficult for children to learn how to process. One of the best ways you can help support your foster/adoptive child with their intrusive symptoms is to help normalize the feelings. By providing a supportive and empathetic understanding that these kinds of intrusive thoughts are normal can help lead your child to accept their thoughts without judgment. It can be beneficial for your child to learn mindfulness techniques to watch their feelings and thoughts come and go without judging them. This is one reason why it is important to find a well-trained therapist to help your child learn how to respond to intrusive symptoms.

Avoidant Symptoms

A third cluster of symptoms related to trauma are avoidant symptoms (APA, 2013). Avoidance is a protective measure. When a child avoids, he/she is protecting themselves from the possibility of getting hurt.

Therefore, avoidance is a self-protective mechanism we often do to prevent the uncomfortable feelings associated with thinking or reflecting about our trauma. Unfortunately, it has been shown that one's avoidance patterns will only maintain one's anxiety and trauma symptoms. A child with a trauma history may have the natural tendency to avoid triggers and reminders of the trauma. Therefore, it is important to find a trained therapist to help your child process his/her emotions and thoughts regarding his/her trauma narrative. Some children may have difficulty remembering some key features of their trauma narrative. Sometimes, children will avoid relationships with their caretakers and/or friends. The result can be feeling isolated. Although your child may crave attachment and relationships, it may also bring up fears of hurt and rejection. So, if your child is pushing you away, you can understand that this is a self-protective measure they use to prevent themselves from getting hurt again. It is hard to be patient when you have a child that pushes you away, but I know it is possible for a breakthrough to occur. It happened for my kids after a year or so into the placement! I will never forget the first time my son and daughter called me "daddy".

Arousal and Reactivity Symptoms

The last cluster of symptoms impacts a child's arousal and reactivity. This includes symptoms of physical and emotional reactivity (including behavior outbursts), hypervigilance, irritability, or aggression, increased startle response, risky or destructive behaviors, sleeping problems, difficulty concentrating, depersonalization, and derealization (APA, 2013).

Hypervigilance is very common for children with a history of trauma. As a result of their experiences, many children with a history of trauma will constantly be looking for danger and threats around them. Our kids will interpret their sensory input from their brains based on their prior experiences. Unfortunately, traumatized children may also misinterpret the cues. For example, your child may be in a safe environment with you; however, they may constantly look for possible threats around them. This may be evidenced by asking lots of questions about what is going to happen next. It could also result in your child being quite anxious or resistant about going to new places or experiencing new things. Your child's brain may always be looking for threats (whether real or threat) and constantly be on alert, especially in new environments. Their brains tell them that threat is just around the corner!

Trauma symptoms can result in attention-related problems. Some children with a history of trauma are incorrectly diagnosed with attention-deficit/hyperactivity disorder (ADHD) when they just only have PTSD. The reason is that one of the symptoms of PTSD is a challenge in being able to focus and concentrate. In addition, many children with trauma backgrounds may experience challenges with sleeping.

Depersonalization and derealization sometimes occur for children with a history of trauma. Depersonalization occurs when one feels detached from their body. Many therapy techniques involve helping children become more aware of their bodies and their space. In addition, some children with trauma histories experience derealization. This occurs when one has experiences while questioning the reality of the experience. Many children with a trauma history may have difficulty in distinguishing reality from make-believe as they have learned to protect themselves by shutting off some of their senses when they experience things such as physical, sexual abuse, or neglect. When this is repeated over and over, it can result in derealization. This is also why some children may remember certain trauma cues and yet not recall other key features related to their trauma. One of my children used to say things like, "Is this really happening?" or "Is this a dream?". This derealization was a symptom of his trauma history.

Early trauma can disrupt a child's metabolism as well as the hormones that govern one's appetite. Therefore, they may be more prone to overeating. In addition, children with trauma histories are more prone to developing addictions to alcohol and drugs when they get older.

Dr. Stephen Porges introduced the concept of neuroception. Neuroception is what our nervous system and brain do very quickly to determine one's safety. He used a term called polyvagal safety A person's brain is continually and quickly interpreting the stimuli around them to determine the risk and safety of their immediate environment (Porges, 2004, 2021). Sometimes our kids will engage in certain behaviors when perceived threat becomes imminent. When you tell your child who has been adopted that they cannot have a snack, boom fear is activated within their nervous system! When you respond with a "no", bam their nervous system reacts (and quickly)! Notice, there may not be any threat, but for many of our kids under our care, their experiences and nervous system constantly result in fear and disruption of a sense of safety. For a child with a trauma history, it causes one's brain to quickly make judgments about their safety, but often, they may misinterpret the cues around them.

Children with a trauma history may have a wide variety of responses to stressful situations in their lives. Traumatized children will likely experience frequent emotional dysregulation and have difficulty responding to disappointments, changes, and/or restrictions. Some children may become quite reactive and lash out at others when they feel threatened or fearful. Other children will become quite shy and withdrawn at the first sign of stress. One child may shut down and another child may lash out with violent and aggressive explosions. The reason for these differences lies in the way that our brain and body respond to stress and trauma.

To survive a life-threatening or frightening, stressful experience, our neurological system will experience a "fight, flight, or freeze" response as a functional protective measure. The amygdala is the part of the brain that detects fear and initiates the "fight, flight, or freeze" response in our bodies. The amygdala is part of the limbic system of the brain which processes fears and emotions. This response happens very quickly (without thinking). It is designed to be quick. It is not designed to be thoughtful and deliberate. In fact, when the limbic system is activated, it short circuits the frontal cortex (the thinking and rational part of the brain). Therefore, children who are in a state of fear or stress are unable to think or rationalize in their bodies as all the resources of their neurological system are seeking to simply survive a threat. When a child is stressed, our bodies release adrenaline (epinephrine) and cortisol. Adrenaline is a stress hormone that can give your child a boost of energy and physical strength. Adrenaline increases the blood circulation and breathing in the body and initiates the fight, flight, and freeze response of the body. The effects of adrenaline can last several hours after a stressful situation. Cortisol also is a stress hormone that affects body processes and regulation. For example, cortisol will help make your heart beat faster and help to increase glucose in your muscles so your muscles can have extra energy. Unfortunately, if your child experiences chronic stress over a long period of time, the increased levels of cortisol and adrenaline can cause health-related problems including heart disease and diabetes. Neurodevelopment research shows that traumatic stress results in increased cortisol levels and adrenaline, and these increased levels can result in damage to your child's brain. This increased level of toxic stress can result in fewer neurons in your child's brain and can also result in a constant fight-or-flight state for your child. It has been shown that repeated exposure to toxic stress can change the function and structure of your child's brain (Blankenship et al., 2019). In addition, cortisol and adrenaline can impact a baby even before birth. If the birth mom is highly stressed during pregnancy, her stress hormones such as cortisol can pass to the infant in the womb. This exposure can stunt the development of neurons in an infant's brain (Lautarescu *et al.*, 2020).

Fight response

Your child's body may respond in a "fight mode" to stress by lashing out. Fight responses may include becoming aggressive such as kicking, hitting, or throwing things. You can probably imagine a situation in which a child who is *dysregulated, fearful, or angry might* become reactive and engage in physical aggression

When this occurs, adrenaline is released in our body and our heartbeat and muscle movement will increase. Often, this results in externalizing behaviors such as aggression and irritability. Your child may instinctually become aggressive with behaviors such as hitting, kicking, or being verbally disrespectful. This may be a type of instinctual survival response. It likely is a quick response that likely results in a burst of energy due to the sudden release of cortisol and adrenaline in their bodies. The goal is to protect themselves from their brain's interpretation of pending harm. Remember, that their brain interprets sensory information based upon prior experience and the imprints of their historical experiences. They may be safe, but their brain and body tell them otherwise.

Flight response

On the other hand, your child can also "flee" or run away from stress. This may include behaviors of running away or leaving a situation. Like a fight response, the flight response is a self-protective response. Your child may seek to flee the threat to get to a safer place. For young children, you may notice signs of anxiety

Freeze response

For some children, especially, when it is not possible for them to escape, their bodies basically shut down or "freeze". Freeze responses from our children may include tuning out stimuli in the environment or even whining or engaging in clingy behavior.

They disassociate from their surroundings to protect themselves as they are unable to escape. Your child may seek to check out from their environment to protect themselves from the harsh reality at the moment. Your child may also seek to hide their feelings as a freeze response. Over the long term, a child may learn to isolate themselves. Others may use fantasy and their imagination to escape the ongoing stresses in their environment. Again, this is a self-protective measure that our brain and body will adjust to stress in times in which it is not possible to escape the situation. Instead of releasing adrenaline, their bodies release opioids (enkephalins and endorphins) to help deal with pain as their heartbeat decreases. The release of opioids from disassociation can become quite soothing as well. When this happens frequently, some children with trauma will learn to disassociate to experience the pain reduction and even pleasure that opiates can bring them. Since our bodies can respond to threats in different ways, it can be easier to understand how your child may engage in a wide range of behaviors in response to stress (Perry & Winfrey, 2021).

The fawn response

The fawn response is a term coined by Peter Walker. This response is also a self-protective response. A fawn response occurs when a child seeks to please or pacify a potential abuser to maintain safety (Walker, 2013). A child may abandon their own needs and focus on overly pleasing others to avoid displeasure or criticism or conflict. This may be evidenced by children who constantly apologize to others as well. Over time, this can even lead to codependency and an individual who has a difficult time with self-care and establishing personal boundaries.

It is important to understand the following districntion. The flight, fight, freeze response are innate, reactive, and neurological responses to stress. These behaviors are considered respondent behavior that are elicited by antecedent stimuli (rather than learned). However, the fawn response is a learned behavior (operant behavior) based upon the consequences that follow the behavior.

Your child's limbic system in their brain is designed to keep your child safe, but their experience results in that part of their brain going overboard to always being fearful. The good news is there is growing research that shows that a child's limbic circuitry and neural networks can and do rewire, especially as trust and attachment are built! This is referred to as the plasticity of the brain, which is the brain's ability to reorganize itself in both structure and function (Bennett et al., 2018). You can read more about some of the neurobiological research in chapter four.

FIGHT	FLIGHT	FREEZE	FAWN
Your child may lash out by being verbally or physically aggressive. Their body releases cortisol and adrenaline.	Your child may attempt to run away, retreat, hide, or isolate. Their body releases cortisol and adrenaline.	Can include physical, social, emotional, or spiritual consequences. Their body releases opioids to help deal with pain and may disassociate from reality.	Your child may seek to please the abuser to maintain safety. He/she may excessively apologize to the abuser.

Figure 2.3 Fight, Flight, Freeze, Fawn Response

Perry & Winprhey (2021) highlight that a healthy nervous system occurs when the stressor is predictable, moderate, and controllable (rather than unpredictable, severe, or not controllable). In addition, a child will develop a healthy resilient stress response system when their caretakers provide frequent, consistent, and predictable measures of comfort and soothing when their child is dysregulated. When this occurs, it helps to facilitate healthy brain development. Unfortunately, early trauma can hinder healthy brain development when their brains constantly tell them that they are not safe. When your child's stress response cycle is severe and inconsistent due to ongoing toxic stress, it is easy to see how this will likely lead to emotional dysregulation along with all kinds of maladaptive behaviors. For example, your child's meltdowns and oppositional behaviors may simply be a measure of their lack of internal balance in their lives as a result of not always feeling safe. Their behaviors may be a way to protect themselves when they do not feel safe.

There are several things you can do to hel your child deal with the effects of chronic stress. First, it is helpful to understand the fligh to understand the flight and fight response. Secondly, foster and adoptive parents validate their child's emotions and feelings. Provide empathy and be active in affirming your child's experiences. Thirdly, providing structure and predictability sets the stage where your child can learn to trust you. It is important to do a lot of planning for transitions, so your child does not become surprised by unexpected things. Fourthly, it is important to model and teach regulation skills and coping skills such as taking deep breaths to learn to respond to various triggers and stress.

Robyn Gobbel highlighted,

> *The crucial time period in an infant's first 18 months of life creates a map for relationships. When babies experience safe, predictable, and loving caregiving, they learn to expect relationships to be safe, predictable, and loving. This impacts the kinds of relationships the child seeks out in the future. (Gobbel, 2024, p. 31)*

As a trauma-informed foster parent, it is important for you to realize that your child's trauma will likely result in difficulties with attachment and bonding. And this avoidance of attachment is functional! It serves as a function of escape from potential harm (at least as their nervous system and brain tells them). Behind every attempt to push you away is a foundational desire and need for connection. Your child desperately needs and wants connection but may be fearful at the same time. Providing your consistent support and empathy (especially at the time of your child's dysregulation) will help facilitate your child's ability to attach to you.

Your child may also be resistant to your comfort and/or touch. Others may be extra clingy and will not want you to leave them. Trauma can also result in social delays. Many children with trauma histories feel alone and isolated. They may seek to withdraw from others because it can be so triggering for them to be around certain social situations. On the other hand, they may be extra bossy and controlling in their relationships as well.

The developmental trauma that our kids have endured will likely impact their ability to attach to new caregivers, especially if they have been ripped apart from their birth/first parent. It is quite possible that your child will attempt to push you away by their words and behaviors. This is a self-protective behavior to try to prevent themselves from getting hurt again. Secure attachments between parent and child occur when a parent is attuned and responsive to the needs of their children. If this does not occur, it is possible that your child may have an insecure attachment pattern that results in all kinds of maladaptive behavioral patterns. However, there is hope that your child will begin to trust you, connect with you, and open their tender and beautiful hearts to you as you use empathetic, trauma-informed parenting practices. An insecurely attached child can become a secure attachment with you. The goal is for your child to feel safe, secure, and soothed by your presence and interaction with them.

Children with trauma often display behaviors that may push them away from (not only you) but also their friends. Many children with trauma histories try to control all aspects of their environment, which may mean that your child struggles with certain friendship skills such as:

- Sharing
- Flexibility
- Compromising
- Showing empathy for their friends

In addition, many children with trauma histories will resort to aggressive behaviors that will certainly alienate them from their peers. It is important to help your child learn new friendship-seeking skills. Often, children with trauma histories simply need to learn new skills and behavioral patterns related to interactions with others.

It is important to understand that a child's early experiences impact the brain, The brain develops based upon the experiences.

It is true that behavioral patterns and experiences can change the brain. That is what is referred to as a "experience dependent" brain. The development and reorganization of the brain is dependent upon one's experiences. For example,

---

Children who have experienced deprivation early in life tend to have brains that do not regulate emotions well. They over-react and under-react in a way that is adaptive to their old environment. When they are nurturing, comforting, and positively stimulating, parents give children experiences that form a new perceptual map. (Gray, 2012, p. 275)

It can be quite depressing to consider all the types of symptoms that your child may experience or will experience. I certainly hope that you are not tempted to put the rest of the book away as it can be quite overwhelming to reflect upon such a difficult topic. However, when you can be a consistent and attuned trauma-informed foster parent, it will help you to create an environment where your child can move from surviving to thriving!

When you can have empathy and compassion for your child when they unleash a volcano of emotions, it will help facilitate greater attachment with your child. In addition, relationships and connections can alter the brain (Perry & Winfrey, 2021). Understanding the effects, impact, and symptoms of childhood trauma can significantly improve the outcomes of children. Your child's nervous system and brain can change for the better. The main ingredient for this change is through connected relationships. When your child who is in foster care is dysregulated, this is the best way to bring healing to your child's brain by providing him/her with consistent and liberal amounts of empathy, comfort, and support. Don't give up!

There is hope! Stable, loving, and healthy relationships can help bring healing to your child and reduce the symptoms of trauma.

The beginning of this chapter might feel a bit depressing, but I want to end this chapter with a hopeful insight which is amazing! The good news is that connection and stability in relationships can help cure some of the symptoms discussed. The connection that you have will help provide an environment for your child to learn new behavioral patterns. Attachment between caretaker and child can and does help restore the functioning of your child's brain!

Even though your child in foster care may have stunted development due to their trauma, your child's cognitive, social, and emotional development can blossom over time! It takes a lot of positive interactions. It takes having a lot

*of conflict that is resolved in a peaceful manner.
It takes a parent who can provide understanding
and support during a meltdown. What is broken
and fractured can be restored. Trust has been
shattered, but your child can trust again. Healthy
relationships are the key to resiliency!*

It takes a lot of patience for these things to happen. Please do not lose hope! Over time, your child will hopefully grow and develop more healthy belief systems and develop a new behavioral repertoire as you implement the strategies that are discussed in the remaining chapters.

Lessons Learned

1. There is a wide range of symptoms and behaviors associated with childhood trauma. It is important to remember that sometimes your child's behavioral symptoms are normal and reactive responses to the stress in their lives. This understanding can help you to be more patient and empathetic when chaos erupts in your household.
2. Although trauma can impact all areas of functioning for your child (developmentally, emotionally, behaviorally, academically, and cognitively), please do not forget that healthy attachments over time can also impact all areas of functioning for your child in a positive way.
3. The flight, fight, and freeze response is quick and automatic. A child may lash out with their behaviors when they are fearful. Fear short circuits the thinking part of the brain. An empathetic response is the best way to get a child to move from the amygdala and fearful part of their brain to the thinking cortex part of their brain. It may seem counterintuitive to show empathy and seek connection when a meltdown occurs; however, this approach just sets the stage to help your child to be able to process their emotions when fear has subsided.
4. A strong connection with a caretaker/parent is one of the best ways to rewire the brain of a traumatized child.
5. Trust takes time to build, especially for survivors of trauma.
6. When you feel like giving up, take one day at a time. Remember, the positives and the small steps of growth and progress you see in your child.

References

American Academy of Pediatrics. (2020). Developmental Issues for Young Children in Foster Care. *Pediatrics*. 106 (5), 1145–1150.

American Psychiatric Association. (2013). *Diagnostic and Statistical Manual of* Mental Disorders (5th ed.) https://doi.org/10.11.1176/appi.books.9780890425596.

Beck, A., Rush, J., Shaw, B.F., & Emery, G. (1987). *Cognitive Therapy of Depression*. Guilford Press.

Bennett, S.H., Kirby, A.J., & Finnerty, G.T. (2018). Rewiring the Connectome: Evidence and Effects. *Neurosci Biobeh Rev*. 88, 51–62.

Blankenship, S.L., Botdorf, M., Riggins, T., & Doughherty, L.R. (2019). Lasting Effects of Stress Physiology on the Brain: Cortisol Reactivity During Preschool Predicts Hippocampal Functional Connectivity at School Age. *Dev Cogn Neurosci*. 40, 100736.

Bowlby, J. (1969/1982). Attachment and loss: Vol. 1. Attachment. Penguin Books.

Cross, D., Negar, F., Powers, A., & Bradley, B. (2017). Neurobiological Development in the Context of Childhood Trauma. *Clin Psychol*. 24 (2), 111–124.

Dweck, C. (2007). Mindset: *The New Psychology of Success*. Ballantine Books.

Evans, A., & Coccoma, P. (2014). *Trauma-Informed Care: How Neuroscience Influences Practice*. Routledge.

Geng, F., Botdorf, M., & Riggins, T. (2021). How Behavior Shapes the Brain and the Brain Shapes Behavior: Insights from Memory Development. *J Neurosci*. 41 (5), 981–990.

Gobbel, R. (2024). *Raising Kids with Big Baffling Behaviors: Brain-Body-Sensory Strategies that Really Work*. Jessica Kingsley Publishing.

Gray, D. (2012). *Attaching in Adoption: Practical Tools for Today's Parents*. Jessica Kingsley Publishing.

Lautarescu, A., Craig, M.C., & Glover, V. (2020). Chapter Two – Prenatal Stress: Effects on Fetal and Child Brain Development. *Int Rev Neurobiol*. 150, 17–40.

Perry, B.P., & Winfrey, O. (2021). *What Happened to You? Conversations on Trauma, Resilience, and Healing*. Macmillan.

Porges, S. (2004). Neuroception: A Subconscious System for Detecting Threats and Safety. *Zero to Three*, 24(5), 19–44.

Porges, S. (2021). *Polyvagal Safety: Attachment, Communication, Self-Regulation*. W.W. Norton & Company.

Siegel, D.J. (1999). *The Developing Mind: Toward a Neurobiology of Interpersonal Experience*. Guilford Press.

Substance Abuse and Mental Health Services Administration. (2014). SAMHSA's Concept of Trauma and Guidance for a Trauma-Informed Approach. HHS.

Walker, P. (2013). *Complex PTSD: From Surviving to Thriving*. Azure Coyote Publishing.

Utilizing Trauma-Informed Care

3

> Our shift needs to change from "I am here to change your behavior" to "My desire is to understand you, protect you, and love you unconditionally". This kind of relationship that a trauma-informed foster parent develops with their child is the foundational blueprint for trauma-informed foster parenting.

Across disciplines, there is a buzz term for agencies that work with individuals with trauma. School systems, mental health providers, and residential centers use a term called "Trauma-Informed Care" (TIC). The practices of TIC have become the centerpiece of best practices and policy guidelines for care (Baker *et al.*, 2018; Rajarman *et al.*, 2022).

The National Child Traumatic Stress Network defines TIC as care in which "all parties involved recognize and respond to the effects of traumatic stress on children on those who have contact with the system including children, caregivers, and service providers" (National Child Traumatic Stress Network, 2016).

It should be noted that TIC is not just about being informed about trauma. TIC is more broadly achieved when the policies, environments, procedures, and relationships involved are both informed and enacted by a deeper understanding of trauma.

The foundation of TIC involves relationships. It involves empowering parents, foster/adoptive parents, and professionals to form and maintain safe, stable, and nurturing relationships (SSNRs) (Forkey *et al.*, 2021). TIC encourages providers to understand the impact of trauma regarding their patients and to provide empathetic care in the process.

It is paramount that your child stay connected with others. A child who feels disconnected and isolated will struggle with learning age-appropriate social and emotional skills. "In childhood, attachment figures can be a parent, guardian, or a person who helps us feel safe...This emotional bonding and nurturing relationship fosters confidence as we

DOI: 10.4324/9781003601081-5

develop an understanding of our environment" (Evans & Coccoma, 2014, p. 45). The caregiving environment is so important it can even alter the neurochemicals and the systems that impact a child's ability to regulate their emotions (Perry, 2001).

John Bowlby is the pioneer of attachment theory. The premise of attachment theory revolves around the basic need for children to attach to their caretakers. Bowlby (1988) and Fraser *et al.* (2010) highlight how trauma can impact the ways children relate to others. Specifically, it can result in children who find it difficult to attach to their caretakers and become reactive in their relationship with others. Therefore, trauma-informed foster parents (TIFPs) understand the role relationships must play in the recovery and healing process of their foster/adoptive children. Bowlby outlined that children need to establish a "secure base" so that children can feel safe. Safety and attachment are developed when parents meet the needs of their children. Solomon and George (1999) identified that children who do not have a secure base develop disorganized attachment style and view the world as confusing and unpredictable. In addition, they can become hypervigilant toward any perceived threats.

Hobfoll *et al.* (2007) outlined the following five aspects of TIC:

1. Promote safety for the client.
   Obviously, a child with a trauma history has many fears. Our goal will be to help our child experience felt safety within the context of a trusting relationship with you.
2. Promote strategies to help the client learn to stay calm.
   Your child likely needs to learn new skills to express and release their frustrations. Therefore, whenever, your child has a meltdown, there is eventually an opportunity to teach a new skill so your child can learn how to regulate themselves.
3. Teach self-efficacy.
   Self-efficacy is the belief in one's ability to influence events in their environment. Basically, it is a child's belief that he/she can engage in certain behaviors to achieve a particular outcome. We want to help our child have self-confidence in their own strengths and abilities.
4. Encourage people to stay connected with others.

Connection helps toward resiliency; it helps bring healing. This is a primary basis for trauma-informed care. Never lose sight of connection!

---

5. Instill hope.
   Your child needs to know that you believe in them; it is also important for you to have hope that things may get better in the future.
   You may not be able to fix all their problems, but you are certainly
   going to be present with them in their problems. This mindset and
   attitude will, hopefully, instill great hope for their future.

As you can see, these five-part objectives are certainly applicable to
trauma-informed foster parenting (TIFPing). Trauma-informed parenting (TIP) is a term that has been used for parents to provide an understanding of trauma as well as support effective discipline practices for
the traumatized child. Providing safety, stability, and predictability is the
hallmark for TIFPing.

---

*The focus is not on changing behavior, but the
focus in providing a safe, stable, and nurturing
relationship (SSNR). When a child's environment
moves from fear, instability, and toxic to safe,
stable, and nurturing, this shift in the environment
sets the stage for changed behavior.*

The result is changed behavior, but it should not be our primary objective. If changed behavior becomes our primary objective, we will lose
sight of connection during the meltdowns.

TIP is a term used that emphasizes caretakers/parents being sensitive to how to respond in a safe and supportive manner to their child
with trauma, as traditional parenting practices are not often effective with children with trauma histories. Typically, this involves using
positive behavioral interventions as compared to engaging in punitive
punishment-based strategies of child discipline. They usually focus on
teaching and guiding through positive reinforcement as well as utilizing
natural consequences.

SAMHSA (2014) had a seminal article called "SAMHSA's Concept of
Trauma and Guidance for a Trauma-Informed Approach". In the article, they outlined six key principles for a trauma-informed approach for
organizations working with individuals with trauma. These six areas
outlined were safety, trustworthiness, peer support, collaboration,
empowerment/choice/voice, and cultural/historical/gender issues.

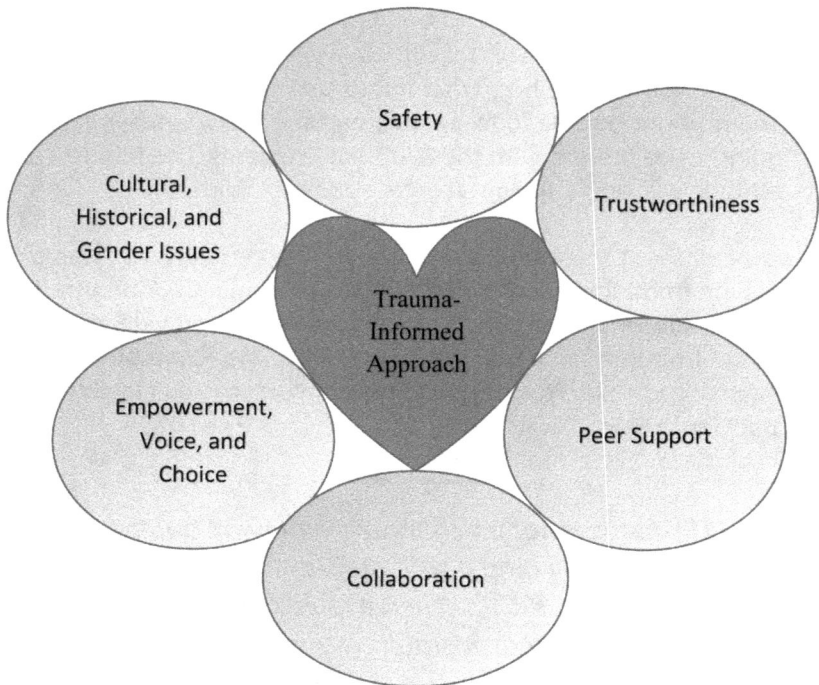

Figure 3.1 SAMHSA (2014) Principles for a Trauma-Informed Approach

These six principles that were developed for TIC can be adapted to apply for TIP. I have coined the term trauma-informed foster parenting (TIFPing) to refer to how foster and adoptive parents can utilize the principles of TIC with their children in foster care. When I refer to the term TIFP in this book, I am referring to both foster parents, adoptive parents, and kinship care.

Safety

A foster parent's prime objective is to provide love and safety for their child.

The priority of a TIFP is to always help their child feel safe and secure. As foster parents, we need to determine any barriers to felt safety. Often, a child with a trauma history has certain fears, so it is important to help support your child in their fears so they can always feel safe. Keep in mind that a child may be safe but may not have perceived safety because of their previous experiences.

It is important to realize that although your child may be safe, it may take a lot of time for your child to be able to perceive their own safety.

A TIFP always keeps safety of their child in mind. Notice, I did not say that the primary role as a foster parent is to change their behavior. The goal is to love your foster/adoptive child, no matter what!

When I approach my sense of urgency to love, I am less likely to get frustrated by the reality of the challenges of responding to their behaviors. I will no longer be seen as a disciplinarian who is simply seeking to change their behaviors yet misses out on connection, love, and safety.

As foster parents, we sometimes think of all the trauma as happening before they got into our home; however, TIFPs own the fact that sometimes we may unintentionally cause trauma for our children with our reactions, our words, our behaviors, and our discipline practices, especially with a child with a trauma history.

Your child is in a safe environment with you; however, your child's brain still may be in a state of perceived threat. When your child feels safe, their brains can develop healthy neurology so they can learn skills to build relationships and connect with you. However, if a child does not feel safe, you will find that there will be many barriers in their ability to connect with you.

It is necessary for you as a TIFP to recognize and be aware of how you may come across to your child. It is not just what you say, but also how you say things. When you get upset, it is important to maintain a relaxed posture and to speak calmly without raising your voice. This will help your child feel safer. On one occasion, I was listening to a recorded video where I was talking to my kids and asking them to do things. I had no idea at the time, but, when I was listening to the video, I realized how harsh I was coming off in giving a simple instruction. It made me become aware of how I was sounding. I never realized that until I watched the

Table 3.1 How To Set Rules

Don't Say	Do Say
No profanity/disrespectful words	Use Respectful Words
No yelling in the home	Use normal voice volume in the home
Don't break the property	Be respectful of property
No hitting	Keep others safe

video. If you are not sure, ask your spouse or close friend who sees the way you interact with your children.

Structure and routines are very important for a child to feel safe. He/ she needs to know what is expected. Predictability and a consistent parenting approach will help you and your child feel safe. It is not just about your child feeling safe. As a TIFP, you may not always feel safe when your child's trauma symptoms interrupt your need for predictability as well! After all, trauma typically is unpredictable, and situations that are unpredictable may remind your child of their trauma. A traumatic experience teaches a child to not trust others or the world. Therefore, it is important for you to help promote and remind your child of your role to help make sure they feel safe. One way to help your child feel safe is to add structure with a few basic house rules that you attempt to reinforce and encourage with all family members. The house rules should primarily be about safety. In addition, it will be best for you to state the rules in the positive and find ways to reinforce them as compared to stating them in the negative and punishing them. This chart provides examples of how to communicate the rules and expectations.

Find ways to reinforce your children when they honor the house rules. You focus on reinforcing the positive (i.e., provide praise for your child/teen when they use respectful words to communicate their frustration).

Trustworthiness and Transparency

A TIFP seeks to build trust with their children at all costs. In fact, your entire family needs to go out of the way to support and build trust with your child in foster care. The child that you care for may not initially trust you based upon their past interactions with adults; however, over time, your child can begin to trust you.

As a TIFP, I have always gone out of my way to avoid any promise or make any statement unless I am certain that I can fulfill it. Also, it is important that a "maybe" response may be interpreted as a "yes" by your child. If my child asks me if they can go over to a friend's house in the afternoon and I am uncertain the friend is available, I may respond by saying, "Wow! That is a great idea. I will check with their parents to see if that is okay and get back to you. I hope that will work out, and I will let you know". If your child in foster care has a history of broken trust, they will not naturally trust you, so TIFPs are in tune with this need and seek to build trust at all costs.

Trust is a type of glue that bonds and holds things together. Trust can only be built upon a lot of positive interactions. Therefore, positive interactions and trust go hand-in-hand to help build upon felt safety for your child.

Perhaps, you can try to find "champions" for your child. During one period of time, I had a child of mine who was really struggling in school, so I encouraged the school staff to find a "champion" for my child (a janitor, librarians, kitchen staff, secretary, etc.) who was simply to build trust with them and only interact with them on positive terms (without having to redirect their behaviors). The "champion" may find special ways to motivate and encourage your son/daughter by giving "high fives" and letting your child know they believe in them! This can be especially important if your child seems to get in trouble all the time. Finding "champions" for your children can go a long way!

Peer Support

SAMHSA defines peer support as any individuals with "lived experiences of trauma, or in the case of children may be family members of children who have experienced traumatic events and are key caregivers in their recovery" (SAMHSA, 2004, p. 11). As you know, it takes a whole village to raise a resilient child. When possible, it is important to surround your child in foster care with any peer, relative, or connection that is invested in your child's recovery. It has been shown that peer support aids in recovery and healing. SAMHSA (2014) outlined the following principles of peer support:

- Voluntary
- Reciprocal
- Non-judgmental
- Respectful
- Direct and honest communication
- Sharing of power
- Mutual responsibility

These same qualities can be embraced by TIFPs.

Collaboration

It is important to collaborate with your child and help them feel a part of decision whenever possible. Mutual decisions can help build trust and create ownership as well. Seeking to create a shared approach with all team members and people invested in your child's life will help create a trauma-informed community. It is important to realize that any one team member will likely not be as effective without the other. It is critical for foster parents to effectively collaborate with their child's schoolteacher.

As children in foster care come with a myriad of emotional issues, many teachers are simply not equipped to handle these issues. Foster children may lash out in the middle of class due to the unfamiliarity and instability of their life at that present time, and many teachers do not have the training or the resources to handle these challenges. Along with this, foster children often

*have difficulty with trust issues when it comes to
adults, as well as building a healthy relationship
with an adult figure. (DeGarmo, 2015, p. 41)*

A TIFP becomes a type of case manager helping to bridge all the systems for the sake of their own child in foster care. It is also important to collaborate with medical professionals including your child's primary doctor, teachers, babysitters, therapists, and others who are invested in your child.

One specific way to collaborate with your child is to schedule family meetings. In the family meeting, you can get input about any concerns that your child may have. In addition, you can discuss ideas for family fun nights, activities, games to play, or future adventures to be planned at the family meetings. Make it a fun time with family nights.

Empowerment, Voice, and Choice

As we seek to empower our children and give them a voice, we facilitate their healing. One way to empower our children is to help provide them with the ability to make ongoing choices in their lives. Many children with trauma histories have a bit of a feisty, oppositional nature. It is part of their way to survive. Consider this as a strength to build upon. Children with trauma backgrounds often have a need for choice and control, so TIFPs seek opportunities to offer more choices to their children whenever possible.

*Their ability to be "in control" is a matter of
survival. Therefore, we can focus on giving
them choice so they can facilitate their ability
to learn, grow, and heal. Otherwise, fear may
creep in through the back door, which will likely
lead to all kinds of behaviors exploding out the
front door!*

Cultural, Historical, and Gender Issues

It is important to take part in your child's culture and incorporate it into your own family whenever possible. In addition, a TIFP seeks to understand their child's history and is sensitive to these experiences. The following are specific ways you can incorporate your child's culture:

1. Increase access to others with similar cultural and historical backgrounds. This is especially important for transracial adoptions.
2. Intentionally seeking mentors who can provide perspectives beyond your own. Be aware of your own cultural bias, so we do not miss the opportunity to strengthen the ethnic/racial identity of your child.
3. Learning about historical trauma of any people group (minority groups) that are part of those who have experienced oppression in the past.

TIFP's can create a healing and nurturing environment while focusing on positive supports to help their child find healing.

Through education, consistency, and support, foster and adoptive parents can help their children grow and thrive by incorporating TIC for their children. In summary, trauma-informed practices require parents to be aware of a child's needs and meet those needs proactively.

What are the needs of my child?

- To feel safe
- To connect and belong
- To be understood
- To feel calm and relaxed
- To be hopeful

What can you do?

- Be predictable
- Be empathetic
- Be nurturing
- Be trustworthy

- Be positive and strength-based
- Help model and teach healthy regulation skills
- Collaborate with others
- Be warm and accepting
- Provide choices
- Listen to their voice

Lessons Learned

1. Choices can help your child feel safe and empowered.
2. Develop family meetings where every child has input and a voice. Family meetings can be a great place to discuss plans, share ideas, and establish a unified agenda. They are also a great place to model compromises and practice skills of giving and receiving.
3. Seek to gain ownership from your child(ren) and help them to be involved in decision-making when possible.
4. Find ways to embrace the culture of your child.
5. For transracial adoptions, surround your child with individuals of the same race and culture when possible.

References

Baker, C.N., Brown, S.M., Wilcox, P., Verlenden, J.M., Black, C.L., & Grant, B.J.E. (2018). The Implementation and Effect of Trauma-Informed Care Within Residential Youth Services in Rural Canada: A Mixed Methods Case Study. *Psychol Trauma*. 10 (6), 666–674. https//doi.org/10.1037/tra0000327

Bowlby, J. (1988). *A Secure Base: Parent-Child Attachment and Healthy Human Development*. Basic Books.

DeGarmo, J. (2015). *Helping Foster Children in School*. Jessica Kingsley Publishing.

Evans, A., & Coccoma, P. (2014). *Trauma-Informed Care: How Neuroscience Influences Practice*. Routledge.

Forkey, H., Szilagyi, M., Kelly, E.T., & Duffee, J. (2021). Trauma-Informed Care. *Pediatrics*. 148(2): e2021052580. https//doi.org/10.1542/peds.2021-052580.

Fraser, J.G., Harris-Britt, A., Thakkallapall, E.L., Kurtz-Costs, B., & Martin, S. (2010). Emotional Availability and Psychosocial Correlates among Mothers in Substance-Abuse Treatment and their Young Infants. *Infant Mental Health J*, 31(1), 1–15.

Hobfoll, S.E., Watson, P., Bell, C.C., Bryant, R.A., Brymer, M.J., Friedman, M.J., Frieman, M., Gersons, B.P., DeJong, J., Layne, C.M., Maguen, S., Neria, Y., Norwood, A.E., Pynoos, R.S., Reissman, D., Ruzek, J.I., Shalev, A.Y., Solomon, Z., Steinberg, A.M., & Ursano, R.J. (2007). Five Essential Elements of Immediate and Mid-Term Mass Trauma Intervention: Empirical Evidence. *Psychiatry*. 70 (4), 283–315.

National Child Traumatic Stress Network. (2016). Fact Sheet: What is Trauma-Informed Child and Family Service System. https://www.nctsn.org/trauma-informed-care/creating-trauma-informed-systems.

Perry, B.D. (2001). The neurodevelopmental impact of violence in childhood. In D. Schetky and E.P. Benedek (Eds.), *Textbook of Child and Adolescent Forensic Psychiatry*. American Psychiatric Press.

Rajarman, A., Austin, J.L., Gover, H.C., Cammilleri, A.P., Donnelly, D.R., & Hanley, G.P. (2022). Toward Trauma-Informed Applications of Behavior Analysis. *J Appl Behav Anal.* 55 (1), 40–61.

Solomon, J., & George, C. (1999). The Place of Disorganization in Attachment Theory: Linking Classic Observations with Contemporary Findings. In J. Solomon & C. George (Eds.), *Attachment Disorganization* (pp 3–32). The Guilford Press.

Substance Abuse and Mental Health Services Administration (SAMHSA). (2014). *SAMHSA's Concept of Trauma and Guidance for a Trauma-Informed Approach.* HHS Publication No. (SMA) 14-4884. Rockville, MD: Substance Abuse and Mental Health Services Administration.

Understanding How Trauma Affects the Brain, Behavior, and Health Outcomes

4

> How devastating it is to know that trauma rewires the biology of the brain; it is liberating to know that connection and stable relationship rewires the brain as well.

This chapter is a bit technical. I hope you can take some time to digest this as it will help you to better understand your child. Understanding the basics of neuroscience will help you recognize how trauma affects the brain, behavior, and one's health. Having this foundation will then assist you in developing a plan on how to respond to behavioral challenges that are so common in children with a history of trauma.

Indeed, trauma affects the brain. First, let's explore a little neuroscience and trauma. A very simplistic way to understand the structure of the brain is to think of the brain as having three main parts: the cortex, the brainstem, and the cerebrum.

The cortex part of our brain involves how we process information. It also affects how we make choices. Our cortex contributes to our thinking/rational processes, our attentional capacity, and our ability to stop impulses based on prior experiences. There are four lobes of the cortex: parietal lobe (sensory processing), frontal lobe (planning, problem-solving, and attentional capacity), occipital lobe (visual processing), and temporal lobe (memory, language, and emotion). The prefrontal lobe of the brain which impacts one's thinking processes, choices, and attention does not fully develop until age 25 or sometimes later due to developmental delays. If you wonder why car insurance is more expensive until the age of 25, it is backed by the science of how the brain develops. The important thing to understand is that the thinking part of the brain is the most effective in the absence of fear, threats, or dysregulation.

DOI: 10.4324/9781003601081-6

The brainstem includes the pons, the medulla, and parts of the mid-brain. These structures impact our temperature regulation, breathing, blood pressure, and heartbeat. This part of the brain is active when your child is in a state of fear as well. It occurs automatically without thinking. It simply reacts to environmental stimuli.

The cerebrum is involved in the coordination of our body movements. It also is involved in things like our balance, posture, and equilibrium. In addition, the limbic system of our brain is a part of the cerebrum. The limbic system includes the amygdala, the hypothalamus, the thalamus, and the hippocampus. The hypothalamus is involved in both our short-term and long-term memories. The amygdala processes our emotions including fear. The limbic system is very reactive and quick. In other words, it takes in sensory information and reacts quickly. It does not "think". The limbic system along with the hypothalamus activates the automatic nervous system, which controls our heartbeat, our breathing, and the fight/flight response.

The thinking part of the brain, including the prefrontal lobe, is not as "quick" as the limbic system. In addition, fear and strong emotion will result in slowing the processes of "thinking". Furthermore, when the limbic system is activated due to fear or strong emotion, the thinking part of the brain becomes short-circuited until the limbic system calms down.

Consider a time in which you got into an argument, and you had emotions that were in high gear. Did you ever say something that you later regret? If you are like me and most others, the answer is an easy "Yes!". Perhaps, there are times in which you react and say some things that you wish you could have taken back. The reason is because if you were high in emotion or fear, you had a type of reactive response where your prefrontal lobe was short-circuited by what was going on in your limbic system. Also, think about a time in which the car in front of you stopped quickly. Did you stop and think, hmm, should I swerve to the right or left? Should I honk my horn? Probably not! Boom! Your automatic nervous system is activated, and you slam on your brakes automatically. Your heartbeat skips a beat and perhaps you notice your breathing patterns change. This is how your limbic system and brainstem operate. They are reactive, and it happens quickly. It does not involve the thinking part of your brain.

Now, for our kids who have repeated exposure to high amounts of stress, they are on "high alert", always looking for threats. This is called hypervigilance. They also may over-interpret threats. They may be in a safe environment with you, but their brain and body are not yet telling them they are safe. Their limbic system may be overly active due to their trauma history.

Have you ever had your son or daughter say, "Quit, yelling at me!" when you were not even yelling at your child? Your child may be misinterpreting the cues around him/her. Perhaps, you had an expression on your face that was misinterpreted by your child. It could be that you had a rigid body posture, and their brain tells them that a rigid body posture means that harm is about to occur. The cue then got interpreted as yelling. Have you ever had your child who is adopted become upset and angry resulting in the overstimulation of certain sounds, noises, or touch? They may be in the middle part of their brain with sensory overload. Indeed, the trauma brain impacts the behavioral patterns of your child.

On one occasion, one of my children had grabbed the television remote from my other child. I took the remote and was going to attempt to do a "re do" in which I was going to ask my child to use their words to request the remote. I raised the remote in the air, and as a result, I accidentally elbowed my child on the shoulder. Due to my child's previous experiences, my child interpreted this in a very different way. My child thought I hit them on purpose. I explained it was an accident and not on purpose, but my child saw it in a completely different way. In addition, in no way was my child able to hear any explanation as this would require their prefrontal lobe when they were operating in the limbic system of their brain. My child exploded in an outburst out of fear by yelling, "You told me you were never going to hit me!!!" My child processed the sensory input on their body through their own trauma lens. You can see how our kids with trauma backgrounds can impact the way they experience various environmental stimuli, and, subsequently, affect their behavioral patterns.

There can be changes in the brain (both structural changes and functional changes) due to repeated stress. Children who are survivors of prolonged stress and adversity experience more microarchitecture changes in their brains as differentiated from adults who are survivors of trauma. These structural changes can "contribute to learning difficulties, impulse control, and mood regulation" (Evans & Coccoma, 2014, p. 49). Structural changes mean that there can be actual physical differences in the structure of the brain. There has been shown to be measurable differences in magnetic resonance imaging (MRI) scans for youth and adults with trauma histories. For example, for individuals with repeated trauma, it has been proven that there are structural changes in the amygdala (the part of the brain that deals with fear and emotions). Changes including an overactive amygdala and an underactive hippocampus can impair the functional aspects of the brain as well. When the amygdala is activated, it will inhibit the activity of the prefrontal cortex, which is the thinking part of the brain (Bremner *et al.*, 2010; Banks *et al.*, 2007; Weems *et al.*, 2015).

Research shows that many individuals diagnosed with PTSD (post-traumatic stress disorder) have a smaller hippocampus than those who do not. Additional research is needed to determine if stress is what causes the changes or if smaller hippocampus causes some people to be more likely to develop PTSD. It could be that a smaller hippocampus makes people more susceptible to the stress associated with adversity (Kim *et al.*, 2015; Yeluda & LeDoux, 2007).

There is preliminary but promising research that shows that the gray matter of the hippocampus can increase in volume following psychological treatment of PTSD. Additional research for this is needed (Butler *et al.*, 2018). The hippocampus is associated with the ability to differentiate time, recall memories, and the ability to understand the difference between the present and the past. It also helps to interpret environmental stimuli in terms of safety or threat. Therefore, the functional purposes of the hippocampus may have some impairment for those who have prolonged exposure to stress (Evans & Coccoma, 2014). Carrion *et al.* (2010) highlight structural changes in the hippocampus may compromise the ability of children to find safety in relationship to their present and historical environment.

We know that many children with trauma histories have reduced volume in their hippocampus and amygdala. Research shows that children who are exposed to violence are more likely to become depressed when experiencing stressful life circumstances. The cognitive and social aspects of the reduced volume in the hippocampus and amygdala increase the vulnerability to stressful life events for children who have experienced violence (Weissman *et al.*, 2020).

In addition to the structural changes in their brain, it has been shown that there are functional changes in the brain for individuals with trauma histories. A functional change means that the functions of the brain change and/or there are differences in the biochemicals of the brain. For example, prolonged stress on a child can have toxic effects on the developing brain. The fear response involves the hypothalamus, pituitary, and adrenal glands also known as the HPA axis. The neurochemicals that are released when a child is in a state of fear can have a toxic effect, especially with repeated and prolonged stress and fear (Evans & Coccoma, 2014). These neurochemicals can have a functional impact on the hippocampus, amygdala, and prefrontal cortex (Rodrigues *et al.*, 2009).

There have been mixed studies on the effects of cortisol levels for youth with a history of trauma and adults with a history of trauma. Some studies show increased levels of cortisol, and others show a decrease in cortisol levels. In a meta-analysis, an interesting finding was that their cortisol levels were lower when there was a long period since the trauma (Miller *et al.*, 2007). Since the adult PTSD studies focus on past trauma, this may explain the inconsistency in the differences in some of the research. Children with more recent trauma histories often have higher cortisol levels; whereas, adults who were survivors of childhood trauma usually have lower cortisol levels as adults (Carrion *et al.*, 2002; Gunnar *et al.*, 2001; Yehuda *et al.*, 1995).

In their study, Carrion *et al.* (2010) found functional changes in the hippocampus for youth when they were processing their trauma memories. They believe that the cortisol released during memory processing may have inhibited the prefrontal cortex, which impacted their ability to process their memory and regulate their emotion.

Chugani *et al.* (2001) examined the positive emission tomography (PET) scans of ten children who were placed in a Romanian orphanage between the ages of 4–6 weeks and remained there for a period of at least 38 months. The researchers found there were functional changes in the amygdala, hippocampus, and the inferior temporal cortex. The results of these reveal functional differences in how the limbic system operated for the kids. The behaviors of these children resulted in emotional dysregulation, challenges in attachment to the adoptive parents, sensory difficulties, and deficits in their ability to play with toys. Developmental language problems were seen in 80 percent of the children as well.

With repeated toxic stress (neglect, physical, sexual, and emotional abuse), children with a history of trauma have been found to have an increase in their cortisol and norepinephrine levels. The hypothalamus sends a signal to the pituitary to signal the adrenal gland to release stress hormones (adrenaline and cortisol). As discussed in Chapter 2, This is also known as the flight or fight system. When children with trauma histories feel overwhelmed, their brains may react with fight, flight, freeze, or fawn response. This system obviously can affect a child's behavioral patterns.

The prefrontal cortex helps to regulate emotions. It is affected by the amygdala. When the amygdala perceives a threat, the prefrontal cortex responds to the threat in more rational ways. However, traumatized individuals may find it difficult to respond rationally and/or may find themselves taking longer to respond rationally. Individuals with trauma histories will often overreact or underreact. Children with a history of trauma have an overactive limbic system. This results in impairment regarding the identification of safety and danger. Furthermore, this can result in one being more susceptible to negative reactions as a first response to stimuli in the environment. Trauma impacts our kids in their ability to adapt to their environment in a calm and safe manner. Therefore, children are likely to experience challenges with emotional regulation and challenges in their ability to focus and pay attention (Liston *et al.*, 2009; Baylin & Hughes, 2016; Forkey *et al.*, 2021).

We know that children with trauma histories often have challenges with emotional regulation. This could be because when the amygdala is activated it makes other parts of the brain such as the prefrontal lobe less active. A heightened amygdala can impact one's ability to regulate emotions. It has also been shown that establishing an environment of safety is a key ingredient to help calm emotions (LeDoux, 1996; Evans & Coccoma, 2014).

Trauma and Health Outcomes

The Adverse Childhood Experiences Study (ACES) occurred in the mid-1990s. The Centers for Disease Control (CDC) and Kaiser Permanente interviewed 17,000 adults as to their exposure to adverse child experiences called an ACE. An ACE included factors such as physical neglect, emotional abuse, sexual abuse, parental mental health, substance abuse, parental separation, and domestic violence. If you were exposed to an ACE, you received a point. These points then were later evaluated to see if there was any correlation between ACES and health outcomes

The results were striking! It was discovered being a survivor of child abuse can significantly increase one's possibility of being exposed to seven out of ten of the leading contributors of death in the US. Childhood trauma can affect the brain system, our hormones, and even how our DNA is read and transcribed (Felitti *et al.*, 1998).

There was a correlated relationship between the ACE score and health outcomes. If one has a higher ACE score, one has a greater risk of a negative health outcome. Felitti *et al.* (1998) identified the following alarming statistics:

- 4 or more ACE – 2.5× risk for chronic pulmonary disease
- 4 or more ACE – 1.9× risk for having cancer
- 4 or more ACE – 2.4× risk for having a stroke
- 4 or more ACE – 4.5× risk- depression
- 4 or more ACE – 12× risk for suicide
- 4 or more ACE – 1.6× risk for diabetes

- 4 or more ACE – 1.6× risk for obesity
- 4 or more ACE – 7× risk for being alcoholic
- 4 or more ACE – 4× risk for using drugs
- 7 or more ACE – 3× risk for lung cancer

Repeated stress can alter a child's immune system. This can result in symptoms including the following: decreased appetite, fatigue, mood changes, irritability, and poor cognitive functioning (Forkey *et al.*, 2021).

Nadine Burke Harris (2018) discussed various behaviors or buffers that people can do that prevent some of the medical and biological harms caused by ACES. Some of these behaviors include accessing mental health care, practicing mindfulness, using stress reduction techniques, exercising regularly, developing good nutrition habits, maintaining adequate sleep, and developing healthy social interactions. These behaviors can help mitigate the effects and symptoms associated with trauma (Purewal *et al.*, 2016, pp. 10–17; Harris, 2018; Kolu, 2023). Kolu (2023) advocates that providers can help create better health outcomes by addressing the barriers for individuals to access the buffers previously highlighted. Extending from Kolu (2023), part of the role of a trauma-informed foster parent (TIFP) is to help ensure their child has access to the buffers to help reduce the effects of trauma in their lives.

There is some good news! The brain science shows that that the brain has neuroplasticity. In other words, the brain can learn to be calmed from stress over time through healing, stable, calm, and connected relationships. This is what trauma-informed foster parenting is all about. The ability to help regulate your child in his/her behaviors.

The main goal of trauma-informed care is to provide stable, healthy, connections so your child can find healing.

- The WAY to do this is to be calm and to co-regulate your child when they are dysregulated.
- The RESULT will be that your child brain begins to feel safe and less reactive.

This may take some time.

LOVING CONNECTIONS CAN REWIRE THE TRAUMA BRAIN. THIS IS NOT GOOD NEWS; IT IS GREAT NEWS!!!!

> ### Lessons Learned
>
> 1. Understanding the neurobiology of trauma can help you to become more patient and empathetic to your child's behaviors.
> 2. It takes time for your child's brain to be rewired to feel safe, heard, and connected. Remember this when you are about to throw the towel in.
> 3. When your child is in a high emotional state of fear or anger, your child thinking capacity will be impaired. The teachable moment will come later. Show empathy and connection first and provide few words.
> 4. Although trauma can impact health outcomes, the connection and stability you offer your child will also bring healing and restoration for your child's body, mind, and emotions.

References

Baylin, J., & Hughes, D.A. (2016). *The Neurobiology of Attachment-Focused Therapy: Enhancing Connection and Trust in the Treatment of Children and Adolescents*. W.W. Norton and Co.

Banks, S.J., Eddy, K.T., Angstadt, M., Nathan, P.J., & Phan, K.L. (2007). Amygdala Frontal Connectivity During Emotion Regulation. *Soc Cogn Affect Neurosci*. 2 (4), 122–147.

Bremner, J.D., Hoffman, M., Afzal, N., Cheema, F.A., Novik, O., Ashraf, A., Brummer, M., Nazeer, A., Goldberg, J., & Vaccarino, V. (2021). The Environment Contributes More than Genetics to Smaller Hippocampal Volume in Posttraumatic Stress Disorder. *J Psychiatr Res*. 137, 579–588.

Butler, O., Willmund, G., Gleich, T., Gallinat, J., Kuhn, S., & Zimmermann, P. (2018). Hippocampal Gray Matter Increases Following Multimodal Psychological Treatment for Combat-Related Traumatic Stress Disorder. *Brain Behav*. 8 (5), e00956. https://doi.org/10.1002/brb3.956.

Carrion, V.G., Weems, C.F., Ray, R.D., Glaser, B., Hessl, D., & Reiss, A.L. (2002). Diurnal Salivary Cortisol in Pediatric Posttraumatic Stress Disorder. *Biol Psychiatry*. 51, 575–582.

Carrion, V.G., Haas, B.W., Garrett, A., Song, S., & Reiss, A.L. (2010). Reduced Hippocampal Activity in Youth With Posttraumatic Stress Symptoms: An fMRI Study. *J Pediatr Psychol*. 35 (5), 559–569.

Chugani, H.T., Behen, M.E., Muzik, O., Juhasz, C., Nagy, F., & Chugani, D.C. (2001). Local Brain Functional Activity Following Early Deprivation: A Study of Postinstutionalized Romanian Orphans. *Neurolmage*. 14 (6), 1290–1301.

Evans, A., & Coccoma, P. (2014). *Trauma-Informed Care: How Neuroscience Influences Practice*. Routledge.

Forkey, H., Szilagyi, M., Kelly, E.T., & Duffee, J. (2021). Trauma-Informed Care. *Pediatrics*. 148 (2), e2021052580. https://doi.org/10.1542/peds.2021-052580

Gunnar, M.R., Morison, S.J., Chisholm, K., & Schuder, M. (2001). Salivary Cortisol Levels in Children Adopted from Romanian Orphanages. *Dev Psychopathol*. 13, 611–628.

Harris, N.B. (2018). *The Deepest Well: Healing the Long-Term Effects of Childhood Adversity*. Bluebird.

Felitti, V.J., Anda, R.F., Nordenberg, D., Edwards, V., Koss, M.P., & Marks, J.S. (1998). Relationship of Childhood Abuse and Household Dysfunction to Many of the Leading Causes of Death in Adults. *Am J Prevent Med*. 14 (4), 245–258.

Kim, E.J., Pellman, B., & Kim, J.J. (2015). Stress Effects on the Hippocampus: Critical Review. *Learn Mem*. 22 (9), 411–416.

Kolu, C. (2023). Providing Buffers, Solving Barriers: Value-Driving Polices and Actions That Protect Client Today and Increase the Chances of Thriving Tomorrow. *Behav Anal Pract*. https://doi.org/10.1007/s40617-023-00876-z

Liston, C., McEwen, B.S., & Casey, B.J. (2009). Psychosocial Stress Reversibly Disrupts Prefrontal Processing and Attentional Control. *Proc Natl Acad Sci USA*. 106 (3), 912–917.

Miller, G.E., Chen, E., & Zhou, E.S. (2007). If It Goes up, Must It Come Down? Chronic Stress and the Hypothalamic–Pituitary–Adrenocortical Axis in Humans. *Psychol Bull*. 133, 25–45.

Purewal, S.K., Bucci, M., Gutiérrez Wang, L., Koita, K., Silvério Marques, S., Oh, D., & Harris, N.B. (2016). Screening for Adverse Childhood Experiences (ACES) in an Integrated Pediatric Care Model. *Zero to Three*. 37 (1), 10–17.

Rodrigues, S., LeDoux, J., & Sapolsky, R. (2009). The Influence of Stress Hormones on Fear Circuitry. *Ann Rev Neurosci*. 32, 289–313.

Weissman, D.G., Lamert, H.K., Rodman, A.M., Peverill, M., Sheridan, M.A., & McLaughlin, K.A. (2020). Reduced Hippocampal and Amygdala Volume as a Mechanism Underlining Stress Desensitization to Depression Following Childhood Trauma. *Depress Anxiety*. 37 (9), 916–925. https://doi.org/10.1002/da.23062

Weems, C.F., Klabunde, M., Russell, J.D., Reiss, A.L., & Carrion, V.G. (2015). Post-Traumatic Stress and Age Variation in Amygdala Volumes Among Youth Exposed to Trauma. *Soc Cog Affect Neurosci*. 10 (2), 1661–1667.

Yehuda, R., Kahana, B., Binder-Brynes, K., Southwick, S., Mason, J.W., & Giller, E.L. (1995). Low Urinary Cortisol Excretion in Holocaust Survivors With Posttraumatic Stress Disorder. *Am J Psychiatry*. 152 (12), 982–986.

Yeluda, R., & LeDoux, J. (2007). Response Variation Following Trauma: A Translational Neuroscience Approach to Understanding PTSD. *Neuron*. 56 (1), 19–32.

Section II

Basic Tenants of TBRI®
and Trauma-Informed
Foster Parenting

In this section, we will use the basic framework of Trust-Based Relational Intervention (TBRI®), including empowering, connecting, and correcting principles to provide you with some support to help you learn how to become a trauma-informed parent.

Trust-Based Relationship Intervention is an attachment-based, trauma-informed intervention developed by Dr. Karyn Purvis and Dr. David Cross. TBRI® uses "empowering principles" to help caretakers and foster parents learn how to meet the needs of their children. "Connecting" principles help trauma-informed foster parents (TIFPs) attach and connect to their children. "Correcting" principles give us practical resources to help disarm fear-based behaviors that are common for children with trauma histories (Purvis *et al.*, 2013, p. 362). TBRI® has well-documented support to show the effectiveness of this approach (Purvis *et al.*, 2010, 2013, 2009; Parris *et al.*, 2015; Razuri *et al.*, 2016; Howard *et al.*, 2016, 2017).

DOI: 10.4324/9781003601081-7

Creatively Empowering Your Child   **5**

Children with trauma histories are desperately seeking to find belonging as their brain and body is looking for safety to overcome their fear.

Trust-Based Relational Intervention (TBRI®) introduces empowering principles as a framework to help create ideal circumstances for healing and connection. Empowering Principles are important tools to help bring about safety and a sense of belonging to your foster/ adoptive child. An empowering, trauma-informed parent helps a child feel more in control of their environment as well as internally regulated with their body. Empowering principles are specific things a caretaker or parent does for their child to help their child feel safe by meeting their physical and environmental needs. In short, it is all about discovering and meeting the needs of your child (Purvis *et al.*, 2013, pp. 363–367).

Purvis *et al.* (2013) outlined two different strategies to help empower our kids: physiological (internal) strategies and ecological (external) strategies. Physiological strategies are things you do to help meet the physical needs of your child. Ecological strategies are things you do to meet the environmental needs of your child (Purvis *et al.*, 2013, pp. 362–363). Applied Behavior Analysis provides a framework to look at how to help manage behavior by looking at environmental changes; therefore, an exhaustive look at environmental or ecological strategies will be discussed in greater detail under the framework of applied behavior analysis in chapters eight through twelve. Table 5.1 provides some examples of the physiological strategies outlined by Purvis *et al.* (2013).

DOI: 10.4324/9781003601081-8

Table 5.1 Physiological Strategies

Physiological Strategies
Physical activity
Nutrition
Hydration
Meeting sensory needs

These strategies were outlined by Purvis et al (2013).

Physiological Strategies

The power of exercise and physical activity

Running, playing outside, jumping on the trampoline, and sports all promote healthy brain development. Physical activity has been shown to lower anxiety, lower the effects of cortisol (stress hormone), improve self-esteem and body image, increase social adaptation, and improve overall quality of life (Caplin *et al.*, 2021; Ashdown-Franks *et al.*, 2020). Plan regular opportunities to go on walks and bike rides and go to the parks together. When you are active with your family through exercise and physical activity, it will also help to empower your child. There has been some research that green therapy helps to release serotonin (a neurotransmitter that is involved in positive mood). Green therapy (also known as Ecotherapy) is simply doing physical activities in green places (such as a park). Green therapy has been linked to a reduction of anxiety and stress. In addition, physical activity can release serotonin (a neurotransmitter that impacts mood) to help improve mood. Exercise used as a proactive tool will help your child burn off their excess energy, so they are more relaxed and content (Summer & Vivian, 2018). If your child is quite active, you will need to find more opportunities for your child to play and run around outside. This will also help bring you more sanity as compared to losing your mind when your child causes chaos and disruption when releasing all that excess energy indoors. You will likely find that your child will be more relaxed and calm after exercising and engaging in physical activity. Win!

The power of nutrition, food and hydration

Children need water and hydration on a frequent basis. Even at low levels, dehydration can impact your child's ability to learn and result in maladaptive behaviors. If a child is not properly hydrated, the excitatory neurotransmitters and increase in heart rate and blood pressure may cause all kinds of behavioral challenges in your child (Purvis *et al.*, 2007, p. 204).

Children need to eat balanced meals. Eating healthy foods will help stabilize blood sugar levels in your child's body (Purvis *et al.*, 2007, p. 199). Being "hangry" is a term most of us are familiar with. This occurs when our child in foster care (or even you) gets a bit testy and edgy when hungry. We are more likely to snap or have a meltdown when we are hungry. Our bodies need nutrients, and our blood needs a certain amount of glucose. Being hangry is often the result of our blood glucose levels dropping. It is also important to know that children have smaller stomachs than adults, so they are likely to get hungry quicker than you. I am always amazed of how quick this process can occur for my own children. Try to always have snacks with you when you go into the community.

Trauma-informed foster parents (TIFPs) are aware of how their child's behavior can be impacted when they are hungry or dehydrated. Over the years, I have learned the best way to my kids' heart is through their stomach. Have you ever observed your child get a burst of hyperactive or irritable behaviors when they are hungry? I had to learn to be proactive at making sure my children always have access to food and snacks to prevent chaos from occurring in our home. I was astounded how a small snack can make the edgy, snappy behavior instantaneously subside. This is not unique to my own kids. The hundreds of foster and adoptive families that I have worked with share similar stories with me. As your child matures, I hope you will find that they will grow in their ability to recognize when they need food and even voice that they are feeling "hangry". There is hope for your child!

The power of the senses

The purpose of our five senses (sight, sound, taste, tactile, and smell) is to help alert our body and brain to environmental stimuli. If you were to hear a sound of shattered glass, suddenly, your flight, fight system would be activated. In this case, you may think someone is trying to break into the house. Therefore, you go and get a weapon such as a bat and slowly look for an intruder, but you become relieved when you observe the broken light bulb that had fallen from the light fixture. The sound activates your sympathetic nervous system (which increases your heart rate and causes you to be on extra alert), but the sight of the glass helps kick your parasympathetic nervous system to calm and relax the processes that are going on in your body.

For a child with trauma history, their senses can be all messed up.

Their bodies have trained them to be constantly on the alert for dangers. A child with a history of physical abuse may be extra sensitive to touch, especially when angry. A child with a history of hearing their parents yell may be quite sensitive to certain sounds. All in all, our senses help us to attend to certain stimuli, and they also help us to organize, attend, and even ignore certain environmental stimuli.

As a TIFP, it is important to understand many children with a history of neglect or trauma may have challenges in the way they process the cues in their environment. They may be quite selective regarding certain sounds, tactile pressure, etc. Perhaps, your child may be resistant to hugs, and you think that it is because they do not love you. However, it could be a sensory issue. Perhaps, your child gets fearful every time they see someone who reminds them of their abuser. A TIFP seeks to be attuned to the sensory needs of their own child and understands how dysregulation can be the result of certain sensory feedback. For example, your child may be touch aversive due to early neglect and/or a history of physical abuse. Some children may struggle with physical affection as they do not experience touch, cuddling, rocking, or hugging as young children.

TIFPs can help their children meet their sensory needs. Children with trauma histories often need a variety of physical activities combined with sensory stimulation Crash and bump opportunities are safe ways to get their energy out by running around, jumping, and getting their physical energy out (Purvis *et al.*, 2007, pp. 163–164). Does your child tend to run around aimlessly crashing into people or walls? If so, he may need some structured opportunities to meet this sensory need in a safe environment. Jumping on the trampoline can be a great exercise and allows your child with a trauma history to meet his/her sensory needs. Some kids need more opportunities to explore their tactile needs. Perhaps, allowing them to do artwork on the table with shaving cream will work for them; others may try to avoid touching anything that is slimy or gooey. Every child is different. The burrito wrap is a great activity for kids who like deep pressure. You can roll or wrap your child in a large blanket or comforter and push on their stomachs or backs for pressure.

Over the years, I discovered my son loved deep pressure. If he was feeling overwhelmed, he would often ask me to give him a bear hug. I would wrap my arms around from the back and squeeze the heck out of him. He loved it. Sometimes, when my son was dysregulated with super energy or anger, I would give him a bear hug (we refer to it as the anaconda squeeze), and he would instantly calm his body. It was like a magic touch for him. In fact, he would usually just melt in my arms in the process. Each child likely has their own sensory preferences, so it may require some experimentation for you to determine the type of sensory feedback that can be calming for your child.

Other Strategies

The power of rituals

Rituals are a wonderful tool to help build attachment as well as to help build trust with your child. Rituals have been found to increase the subjective well-being of the participants and increase the sense of family belonging (Fiese *et al.*, 2006). In addition, rituals have been found to decrease anxiety and increase goal-oriented performance. In addition, there is some evidence that rituals can regulate "the brain's response to personal failure" (Hobson *et al.*, 2017).

Some of my favorite rituals with my children (especially when they were younger) were during bedtime. We had rituals which include snuggling in bed and reflecting upon the "highs" and "lows" of the day. I would spend 1x1 time with each child at bedtime and we would connect with each other and play silly games too.

My daughter and I used to have a fun ritual where we would be drinking, and we would accidentally pour water on each other while lying in bed. As crazy as it sounds, there were the sweetest times of connection between Kayla and me as I was trying to build trust, connection, and attachment with her. See the link to the ritual with Kayla (https://www.drdavidadams.com/trauma-informed-foster-and-adoptive-parenting.html). My son and I have a favorite ritual of nighttime prayers. Ask me to rub his forehead with special oils as well as part of my ritual with him. He always would ask me to say the same type of prayer each night with him asking the angels to protect him when he sleeps. I found these have been a great way for my children to feel safer and create attachment and connection as well.

Rituals help increase connection, and connection helps bring safety. Therefore, rituals can be a great way to help calm a heightened emotional state.

Rituals have had a calming effect on my own children. For example, there was a season during his childhood when he got bad migraines at nighttime. His heightened anxiety would then intensify his migraines. I developed a calming ritual with him in which I would roll a small tube oil canister on his temples and his forehead at night in a special way. As I would do this, I would say encouraging and calming and affirming words to him like, "You got this!" and "I am right here with you. We are going to do this together!". If I were to forget to do this, he would remind me. It's not surprising to me that he would sometimes tell me as we snuggled at nighttime before he goes to bed that he did not want me to leave because I always make him feel safe.

Another bedtime ritual that I had with my son was with nighttime prayers. When he was younger, he developed anxiety and always felt that someone was going to get him. I prayed for him every night and would pray that an angel would hover over him and at each corner of the room and under his bed. There were several times that I prayed over him and did not pray for angels to protect him, and he always would remind me to pray that angels would protect him. Once again, our ritual of nighttime prayers was a great way to calm his heightened emotional state.

The power of priming

Transitions can be a nightmare for foster and adoptive parents! How often have you observed a meltdown when you have asked your child to transition from one activity to another? The key to handling transitions is to be proactive. Most children in foster care settings prefer predictability and structure. Unexpected changes may be a reminder of their previous trauma.

Priming is a behavioral tool that we use to help prepare an individual for what is expected. For example, if your children are playing in the swimming pool, we may say, "In 5 minutes, we will be getting out of the pool. I know it will be hard, but I want to thank you in advance for doing this!". Do you see how you can help paint a picture for your child of what you hope and expect to see in a positive manner? You may then give another advance warning of, "Okay, we have one more minute, please do your last-minute splashing of each other". When you can prime a behavior in advance of what you hope to see, it helps to provide a greater chance that you will see the behavior. Also, it is always best to speak about the behavior you want to see as compared to outlining the behavior you do not wish to observe. Be positive!

It is important to empower your child with a trauma history by helping them to believe in themselves. Every child has a seed of greatness. Unfortunately, due to their trauma background, their seed of greatness may not be self-observed by them. In other words, they have this seed that can grow into greatness, but their trauma and life experiences did not provide the right nutrients for them to grow into who they are! Help your child to see their positive traits. Empower your child by showing your foster and adoptive child that you believe in them. My daughter lived in the wilderness in Arizona. I was so proud of how many sacrifices she made while living in the wilderness for over a month. I would like to share with you a video of when I went to the wilderness with her to help remind her of her seed of greatness (see https://www.drdavidadams.com/trauma-informed-foster-and-adoptive-parenting.html on my website).

When you empower your child, you help emphasize their uniqueness, reinforce their strengths, promote self-expression, and build their self-confidence.

Lessons Learned

1. Create lasting and fun rituals to help strengthen belonging and attachment security.
2. Make sure you always have snacks and water in car rides. In addition, it is good for your cabinet to be stacked with nutritious food snacks.
3. Offer food to your child if you have not seen them eat after a period of three hours. If your child starts to become grumpy, food can be a great distraction as well.
4. If your child is getting grumpy, check to see if he/she wants a snack or drink. Always keep extra food in your purse or in the car. This will come in handy!
5. Tune into your child's sensory needs and provide frequent opportunities for your child to have various forms of sensory input.
6. Physical activity is a great way to help burn off the excess energy your child may have. Take walks to the park and encourage your children to run around… a lot!!!!
7. Choices, Choices, Choices! Constantly give choices to your child.

8. Put lots of "Yeses" in your child's piggy bank.

I would rather give more "yeses" and end up with a slightly spoiled but attached child. It will be a lot easier to work with a spoiled, attached child than a non-attached child who is fighting for control to get what they want.

References

Ashdown-Franks, G., Firth, J., Carney, R., Carvalho, A.F., Hallgren, M., & Koyanagi, A. (2020). Exercise as Medicine for Mental and Substance Use Disorders: a Meta-Review of the Benefits for Neuropsychiatric and Cognitive Outcomes. *Sports Med*. 50 (1), 151–70. https://doi.org/10.1007/s40279-019-01187-6.

Caplin, A., Chen, F.S., Beauchamp, M.R., & Puterman, E. (2021). The Effects of Exercise Intensity on the Cortisol Response to a Subsequent Acute Psychosocial Stressor. *Psychoneuroendocrinology*. 131, 105336.

Hobson, N.M., Bonk, D., & Inzlicht, M. (2017). Rituals Decrease the Neural Response to Performance Failure. *PeerJ*. 5, e3363. https://doi.org/10.7717/peerj.3363

Fiese, B.H. (2006). *Family Routines and Rituals*. Yale University Press.

Howard, A.R., Call, C.D., & Purvis, K.B. (2017). *Trust-Based Relational* Intervention. In K.D. Buckwalter & D. Reed (Eds.), *Attachment Theory in Action: Building Connections between Children and Parents* (pp. 143–156). Rowman & Littlefield: Lanham, MD.

Howard, A.R., Parris, S.R., Nielsen, L.E., Lusk, K., Purvis, K.B., & Cross, D.R. (2016). Trust-Based Relational Intervention® (TBRI®) for Adopted Children Receiving Therapy in an Outpatient Setting. *Child Welfare*. 93 (5), 47–64.

Purvis, K.B., Cross, D.R., Dansereau, D.F., & Parris, S.R. (2013). Trust Based Relationship Intervention (TBRI®): A Systematic Approach to Complex Developmental Trauma. *Child Youth Serv*. 34 (4), 360–384. https://doi.org/10.1080/0145935X.2013.859906

Parris, S.R., Dozier, M., Purvis, K.B., Whitney, C., Grisham, A., & Cross, D.R. (2015). Implementing Trust-Based Relational Intervention in a Charter School at a Residential Facility for At-Risk Youth. *Contemp Sch Psychol*. 19 (3), 157–164.

Purvis, K.B., McKenzie, L.B., Kellermann, G., & Cross, D.R. (2010). An Attachment-Based Approach to Child Custody Evaluation: A Case Study. *J Child Custod*. 7 (1), 45–60.

Purvis, K.B., Cross, D.R., & Sunshine, W.L. (2007). *The Connected Child*. McGraw Hill.

Purvis, K.B., Cross, D.R., & Pennings, J.S. (2009). Trust-Based Relationship Intervention TM: Interactive Principles for Adopted Children with Special Social-Emotional Needs. *J Humanist Couns Edu Dev*. 48, 3–22.

Razuri, E.B., Howard, A.R., Parris, S.R., Call, C.D., DeLuna, J.H., Hall, J.S., Purvis, K.B., & Cross, D.R. (2016). Decrease in Behavioral Problems and Trauma Symptoms Among At-Risk Adopted Children Following Web-Based Trauma-Informed Parent Training Intervention. *J Evid Inf Soc Work*. 13 (2), 165–178.

Summers, J.K., & Vivian, D.N. (2018). Ecotherapy–A Forgotten Ecosystem: A Review. *Front Psychol*. 9, 1389.

Connecting Through the Chaos   6

One of the greatest tragedies that a child can endure is the absence or shattering of a connected heart. The kind of experience results in developmental trauma with all kinds of problems; however, the good news is that healing also takes place in the context of connection. Relationships are the key to helping a child learn to learn to trust, bounce back from adversity, and thrive!

TBRI® emphasizes connecting principles. "The connecting principles enable both child and parent to experience the personal and interpersonal behaviors that build truest and lead to secure attachment" (Purvis *et al.*, 2013, p. 307). We know connection is the key, but it is not that easy, especially when your foster/adoptive child lashes out at you with words and behaviors that seem to suggest a lack of desire for connection. However, don't let that fool you! Our kids long for connection.

Foster parenting is one of the highest callings as a parent to invest and share the hurts and pains of your child. Connection brings healing!

Within the first few weeks of being their new parent, one of my children said, "If you really love us, take us back to our previous foster home". After living with me for several years, my child said, "I wish you never adopted me!" Now, these types of exclamations were said in the heat of a moment. Perhaps, when they did not get something, they wanted or when they felt I was being mean. It was a type of knee-jerk response. The limbic system of their brain (the part that reacts quickly without thinking) as a protective mechanism is what is activated. It is important to

DOI: 10.4324/9781003601081-9

understand that when the limbic system of the brain is activated due to stress, it short circuits the thinking part of the brain (prefrontal cortex). Therefore, our goal should be to help our child move from the quick, reactive part of their brain (the amygdala and the limbic system) to the thoughtful, deliberate part of their brain (prefrontal cortex). The way to do this is to show empathy and understanding when they are responding in the fearful limbic system of their brain.

I have had two initial responses when my kids have said these types of comments: lecture/show signs of disapproval or empathize. If I lecture, I run the risk of keeping my son/daughter in the fearful/limbic system of their brain. If I can show empathy and be calm and relaxed, I help facilitate my child to be able to think more clearly. Then I can truly help my child process their behaviors.

A healthy brain can be observed with children who are connected, but, unfortunately, trauma rewires the brain for protection – protection from harm, protection from danger, protection from conflict.

My initial reaction is to feel hurt and rejected as a foster parent. My own adoptive child hates me. When I feel the pain, I tend to respond with some type of statement such as, "That's not okay to say that!" By doing this, my son/daughter already feels a bit of rejection by me and now I intensify their own belief. This does not work. It only creates more barriers between my own child and myself. It creates more hurt and disconnection.

The second option is to try to find some way to identify and agree with the pain, even if that is criticism directed toward you. Albert Ellis in the book "Feeling Great" said it this way,

---

When you defend yourself from a criticism that is wrong, unfair, or false, you prove that the criticism is absolutely valid, and the critic becomes even more convinced that the criticism is valid and justified. This is a paradox. In contrast, when you find the truth in a criticism that sounds completely

> *unfair, exaggerated, or wrong, you immediately put*
> *the lie to rest, and the critic no longer believes the*
> *criticism. This is also a paradox (Beck, 2020, p. 54)*

I outline the following tips for trauma-informed foster parent (TIFPs) to connect with the children under their care.

Connecting Tip #1: No Negative Reactions for the First 20 Seconds

I often tell adoptive/foster parents to allow 20 seconds for their child to have a reaction, cuss, or say mean things without any sign of disapproval. If you do this, this will help your child's nervous system to relax so they can reason and think and have an actual discussion.

On one occasion, I asked a child of mine to stop what they were doing and to go clean his room. They immediately responded, "No! F—you, dad!". My response was something like, "I see you do not want to clean you room right now. That makes sense to me". Within about 10 seconds, my child says, "Fine!" and immediately goes upstairs to clean their room. It just took a moment of protest, a moment of process, for my child to get out of the reactive limbic system of their brain and into their pre-frontal, thinking part of my child's brain. So, the key, don't show signs of disapproval when your son/daughter has a reactive response for at least 20 seconds. In case you were wondering, I certainly had a conversation with my child afterward as to how my child could have communicated their frustration to me in a more appropriate manner and allowed my child to practice that communication with me as well in a "re-do".

Connecting Tip #2: Avoid Lectures

Let's assume that my foster/adoptive child comes home and explains to me that he/she got in a physical fight with a peer at school. My natural tendency as a parent would be to want to dive into a lecture and help my child understand the alternatives of what could have been done to avoid the fight. Let me ask you, when I do this, what am I missing out on? The opportunity to connect with my adopted child in his/her pain or frustration. Going straight to the advice is not trauma-informed, empathetic foster parenting! What noble intentions I may have at times like this, yet, when I do this, I am just missing out on the opportunity to connect with my son or daughter in the chaos. My goal is to create safety in the relationship. My objective is to create an environment so my child would want to talk to me about their hurts and hang-ups. If I am giving advice every time (before showing empathy), they will begin to tune me out as they approach their teen years.

Connecting Tip #3: Aim for Connection in the Chaos

TIFP(ing) is an intentional relationship. You will have all kinds of interactions with your child. The objective of TIFP(ing) is to connect in every interaction, especially when your child is misbehaving. When you are frustrated with your child's behaviors, please don't forget this as an opportunity to connect with your child in the process.

There is an attachment dance that we have with our kids. Some of our kids are quick to the dance of attachment and some of our kids are a bit resistant. Trauma-informed foster parents meet their kids where they are at and join the dance. It takes a lot of patience and a lot of understanding of trauma to experience the sweet beauty of a connected parenting approach. Aim for Connection in the Chaos!

It takes time, but the results will likely pay off for you in the long run. Connection brings healing.

One of the major findings is that in determining someone's current mental health, the history of their childhood relational health- their connectedness- is as important, if not, more important, then their history of adversity. And

for children and youth experiencing trauma,
the best predictor of their current mental health
functioning is their current connectedness....
Disconnection is a disease (Perry & Winphrey, 2021,
pp. 261–262).

Connecting Tip #4: Be Aware of Your Nonverbals

It is critical for you as the foster/adoptive parent or caretaker to be aware of your demeanor when your child is dysregulated. Oftentimes, children with trauma histories will watch your expressions even more than listening to your words.

Therefore, Purvis *et al.* (2013) encourage caretakers to use attunement strategies. "Through verbal and nonverbal nurturing communications between caregiver and child, attunement can be achieved through matching behaviors, eye contact, voice and inflection, body position, and safe touch" (Purvis *et al.*, 2013, p. 370). These types of attunement strategies help build attachment and connection with your child. This form of connection is critical to building attachment with your child as well as foundational to helping your child learn how to self-regulate.

Connecting Tip #5: Be Fully Present and Focus on Quality Time

We have discussed how important it is to connect with our kids when there is chaos around; however, it is equally important to find special ways to spend quality time with your children. If you have many children in your household, it may be hard to find one-on-one time to be with your kids. Sometimes, you can find special one-on-one time with your kids by combining an activity that you already do with a child. For example, when you go to put gas in your car, you can take a long a child. In my household, I have attempted to do a "special treat" once a month where I take either my son or daughter out to eat at their favorite restaurant. If your kids are anything like mine, you will know that the way to their heart is through their stomach!

Connection Tip #6: Change the Story for Surprises

Many children with trauma histories do not like surprises. Surprises can be unpredictable and may remind your child of their trauma history. Surprises may mean that your child feels powerless or not in control, and this can be quite scary for little people. However, I do like to do fun surprises with my kids. It can be exciting and bring life to your family by doing a spontaneous trip on the weekend or a trip to an amusement park as a surprise. Surprises can help create memories. Therefore, I always tried to emphasize positive surprises for my kiddos by doing certain things unannounced like taking my kids out to fun places. My kids used to tell me that they did not like surprises; however, after a while of creating some fun surprises, they soon loved them! Check out this video link (https://www.drdavidadams.com/trauma-informed-foster-and-adoptive-parenting.html) of a special surprise I provided to my daughter on my website. By spending quality time with your children, you will help to build trust with you and help your child to become more attached to you in the process.

Connection Tip #7: Connect by Noticing and Praising

Kids want to be noticed! When you take advantage of everyday interactions by smiling, laughing, giggling, and noticing your child, your child will feel more valued, appreciated, and connected to you. In fact, learning to laugh with your kids is contagious and is good for the emotional health of both you and your child. As a TIFP, if you do not learn to laugh, you will end up eventually either pulling your hair out or crying (especially as your kids transition from young childhood to preteen years and then from preteen to teen years)! Choose laughter!

Roth (2010) highlighted that parents who provide eye-to-eye gaze and smiles become wired to expect positive social interactions with others as they grow up. On the other hand, children who do not have sufficient experiences of positive attention from their caretakers have decreased self-worth and have difficulties in finding pleasure from the interactions with other people. In short, your smiles and eye gaze help to wire the brain and the arousal circuits to find pleasure in social interactions (Archer & Gordon, 2013).

Another great connecting strategy is bragging about your kids individually and to others publicly. Your child likely may suffer from a poor self-esteem due to their trauma history. Find ways to praise their small steps of growth. Remind them regularly about their positive traits. Not only will this help your child change their own view about themselves, but it may also help you change your own view of them! Also, be sure to start this when they are young, but don't stop when they are teens. Your child may show greater resistance when they are older, but they still need to know that you are their biggest fan!

Connection Tip #8: Connecting through Healthy Touch

Touch is one of the most important senses in life. However, children with trauma histories may struggle with touch, so it is important to be aware of how touch impacts your child. Even though your child may be resistant to your touch, your child still needs to have healthy forms of safe and loving touch. Therefore, it is important to respect the boundaries that your child may have regarding touch (Purvis *et al.*, 2007, p. 160).

It is critical for you to ask permission to provide touch to your foster/adoptive child. You may ask, "Is it okay for me to rub your back?" Your child needs to know that their body is their own body, and they always have a right to say "no" to touch that may feel uncomfortable.

Research shows that healthy touch will facilitate a boost of oxytocin. Oxytocin is a hormone that has been associated with social interactions and bonding. It has also been shown to reduce anxiety and stress, improve cooperation, improve sleep, and improve cognitive performance. Touch can help people feel safe, soothed, and secure (Field *et al.*, 1996; Hart *et al.*, 1998). It has also been demonstrated that touch can be seen as more or less reinforcing based on who is providing the touch. The rewarding aspects of touch with oxytocin are tied to the dopamine and opioid reward systems in the brain that further promote bonding. Infant massages are believed to help promote growth and have been used in neonatal units. Research has shown that there is a correlation between early discharge from neonatal units when infant massages are used (Li *et al.*, 2022).

Here are some examples of ways you can use healthy touch with your child:

- Tickles
- Cuddles
- Back rubs or pats on the back

- Massages
- High fives
- Hugs
- Play wrestling
- Swimming/tossing your children in the air
- Sitting in lap (for younger children)
- Piggy-back rides
- Thumb war
- Hand slaps game
- Drawing letters on their back with "Guess the letter" game
- Doing each other's hair

These types of regulating, calming, and soothing experiences will result in increased connection with your child. Healthy forms of touch not only help build connection, but they can also help your child feel loved, accepted, wanted, and build their self-confidence.

Connection Tip #9: Connect through Play

Dan Hughes, an attachment specialist, outlined that parents can use the **P**layfulness, **A**cceptance, **C**uriosity, and **E**mpathy (P.A.C.E.) model to help their children connect through play. This model consists of trauma-informed practices to help parents to connect with their children and help them feel safe. Parents need to engage with their children with P.A.C.E. (Hughes & Baylin, 2012; Golding & Hughes, 2012).

Play is a great way to build attachment with any child with a trauma history. Kids by nature are playful, so it is a great way to join them in their playful nature. Playing silly games with your children can be entertaining. If your child is playing with Legos, take an opportunity to join your child in building with your child. If your child is playing with dolls, get on the ground and play with them. Joint interactive play is when you take a part or role, and your child takes a part in your play together. This can be a great way to connect with your child. My daughter used to love to paint my toenails and fingernails, and you bet I bit my pride and allowed her to paint them at times. My daughter loved to play shop with me, and she would set up a whole store for me to come in and purchase various items. Some of my favorite memories are the special times that I have had the opportunity to be playful and silly with my own kids.

Often, children with a history of rejection will experience rejection when you are seeking to discipline them or seeking to address their maladaptive behaviors. By providing acceptance in the P.A.C.E. model, your role as a trauma-informed adoptive parent is to help your child know and understand that there are no wrong feelings. The key is to validate their feelings (Hughes & Baylin, 2012; Golding & Hughes, 2012).

You don't have to agree with someone to validate their feelings. When you validate your child's feelings, they will be less likely to misinterpret behavioral corrections as personal rejection.

In addition, our kids with trauma histories will likely misinterpret threats; therefore, trauma-informed parents are keenly aware of how our non-verbals can unintentionally trigger and/or retraumatize our children. For example, if your child says, "I hate you!", it will likely evoke all kinds of feelings and behaviors for you.

Option 1:
> You could respond by saying, "That is not okay! Don't be mean!" as we have a harsh-looking frown. Although you have the best intentions in the process, you, unfortunately, run the risk that your child will only hear the following messages:

- "I am a bad kid"
- "I mess everything up"
- "Why can't I do things right?"

Option 2:
> A trauma-informed response will be to validate and accept their feeling in the moment, by being aware of their nonverbals and saying,

- "I understand you are really upset at me right now, and that makes sense to me. Would it help if I were to…." (highlight something you can do to help meet your child's need)
- "I see that you really hate me right now. Is there anything I can do to help you right now?"

Please keep in mind that you are not necessarily accepting the behavior, but you accept their feeling. It is important to highlight that you realize that your child is doing the best they can, and it is a difficult situation. It does not mean that you do not address the behavior as well. Acceptance is all about making sure that you are non-judgmental about any feelings they may experience at each moment. It communicates to your child that you accept them, even though you may not like their maladaptive behavior. It will help you to connect to your child when your child sees you as a safe person to share their feelings, no matter how ugly they may be.

According to Hughes (2012), when you are curious about your child, you will seek to learn about what is important for your child. You genuinely become interested in things that interest them. You ask questions and make supportive comments to help build a greater connection in the process with you. When you are curious, you will be less judgmental and more open to learning about your child's thoughts, feelings, hopes, and dreams.

Empathy serves as a bedrock for building attachment. In addition, the goal of empathy is to help a fearful child move from fear to trust. It helps a child who is in their fearful limbic system to their thinking cortex part of the brain. Their thinking part of the brain is where executive functioning skills allow a child to think through choices before they act. When children are dysregulated and/or fearful, they cannot access logic, reasoning, and make effective decisions. Therefore, they need YOU! In addition, this is precisely why co-regulation is so critically important to healthy brain development.

Empathy is the highway to transport your child children from their limbic system to their cortex.

When you show empathy to your child, your child will feel like you understand their feelings (Hughes & Baylin, 2012; Golding & Hughes, 2012). They will feel seen, heard, and secure! When you are empathetic to your child, your child will know they you understand them. When your children know you understand them, it will break down the barriers that hinder attachment, so the sweet aroma of connection is near. Your child needs to know that they will not experience distress by themselves. You are present! Sometimes offering a simple hug after a hard day and saying, "I am sorry that your friends were mean to you today at school" can go a long way to help build greater attachment with you and your child.

It can be hard to display empathy when your child is having a meltdown. It certainly may even be triggering to you. In fact, emotions are contagious. It's easy to catch an emotion. Therefore, it is important for all parents to take really good care of themselves. If you're easily triggered into distress or anger, you will be unable to access your own empathic response when your child needs you the most. However, try to put yourself in your child's perspective and show empathy in the moment. Once your child is calm down, you can process with your child about alternative ways to express their frustrations. However, empathy is the way to get them to the point where you can process, reflect, plan alternative behaviors, and practice re-do's with your child.

Connecting Tip #10: Be Creative in Finding Opportunities to Connect

> Be creative in finding special ways to connect with your child. Take opportunities to share fun experiences like going out in the rain and jumping in the puddles.

Some children with trauma histories may struggle in hearing a lot of praise or positive things about themselves, even though they need to hear it. The moment you say, "Great job!", you may see a downward trajectory of maladaptive behaviors. Right after you say, "Wow, you have been getting along with your sister so well", you see a fight immediately break out. Sound familiar? It probably takes a lot of work and effort to maintain the expectations of being "good" all the time. From your child's perspective, it may be seen as a lot easier to be the troublemaker or instigator around your household. As a result, the moment you praise your child, disruption in the household is soon around the corner. If this is the case with your child, you can periodically take a mental picture of what your child is doing and commenting upon what you notice and observe. You can say things like, "I see you playing with your toys. Looks fun!" This is a way you can remind your child that you are noticing them and that you care without taking a more directive approach of providing them with praise.

Connecting Tip #11: Say "Yes" More

When you say "yes" more to your child, you will help empower your child and increase your connection with your child. On the other hand, Siegel and Bryson (2019) highlighted that hearing "No" a lot can affect the brain in negative ways. They highlighted that children who get a lot of "Yes" tend to have a more positive outlook on life; however, children who hear a lot of "no" tend to shut down emotionally. These children who have a "Yes brain mindset" will see challenges as obstacles that they can overcome. They also highlighted that it can be difficult for children to learn new experiences and show psychological flexibility if they experience a lot of "no's" in their lives (Siegel & Bryson, 2019).

When you say "No" to your child a lot, it is like you are sending them away. What we know is that saying "Yes" helps build attachment. When we constantly say "No", it is a way to distance ourselves from our foster/adoptive child. When they are in a place of distress, you want them to come to you, not someone else. If you are always saying, "no", your child will learn to go to someone else who will say "yes", even if it involves them doing drugs or alcohol or having sex. Our kids are craving attention and acceptance. Unfortunately, there are people who will give lots of "Yesses", but they may not be the people you want your child/teen to be around.

On occasion, our family does a "Yes Day". We got the idea after watching the comedy movie "Yes Day" about parents who had to say "Yes" to their kids, no matter what. Well, when we do "Yes Day", I have a few rules. I set a reasonable budget, and I highlight that I cannot say "yes" to anything that will carry over to the next day. That prevents me from doing something like buying them a new pet. Well, my kids absolutely love "Yes Day", and quite honestly, I do too! It is a blast and a great way to bond. Watch this video of our "Yes Day" (https://www.drdavidadams.com/trauma-informed-foster-and-adoptive-parenting.html).

As parents, we, unfortunately, can be attuned to finding and pointing out everything wrong with our child, rather than speaking of what things could be. Does your teen believe you are for them or against them? Or does your child know more about what you like about them or more about what you disapprove of them? As parents, it is important to emphasize more about the things you like about them as compared to the behaviors that you do not like.

***

Let's strive to help our kids know more of what we are for as compared to what we are against. The best way to do this is to reinforce the behaviors that we like to see as compared to show signs of disapproval for the behaviors we do not like to see.

***

Sometimes, You May Find a Way to Say "Yes" When You Would Normally Say "No"

See the following example.

Situation One:

KAYLA   "Can I have some more ice-cream?"
ME   "No!"

Situation Two:

KAYLA   "Can I have some ice-cream?"
ME   "Yes, of course! I would love to eat some ice-cream with you. I know you probably want some now; however, we can plan on getting some tomorrow after lunch. How about we go tomorrow Baskin Robbins together?"

Aim for situation two. It is a way to avoid having to say "no" and at the same time a way to build connection with your child. Think of each child as having a piggy bank. We need to put a lot of "Yesses" in their piggy bank. Saying "Yes" to your child is one of the greatest ways to build attachment with your child.

Behaviorally speaking, when you give a lot of "Yesses" to your child, you set yourself as a conditioned reinforcer. In other words, they will want to be around you more. When they see you, they will have positive, loving feelings toward you. In contrast, if you constantly say, "no", you may unintentionally create a situation where they have negative feelings toward you. Now, when they see you, they will not want to spend as much time with you.

You may think, "Oh, but I don't want to spoil my child who is in foster care". Obviously, you cannot always provide a "yes", and your child will need to learn to accept "no", but the only way they learn to accept a "no" is if they have a lot more "Yesses" in their piggy bank. So, start with the "Yes" as much as possible to build attachment. As attachment develops, you will naturally be providing "no's", but they will be in a much better place to accept a "No".

You may not always be able to give a "Yes". In some situations, you can help empower your child to negotiate when they seem dissatisfied with a request. For example, if your child is upset because they must leave their friend's house, you can prompt your child to request an additional 10 minutes in a calm and respectful manner. This type of negotiation can help to empower your child to find their voice and even be more satisfied. The result is that you also are attempting to maintain connection rather than create frustration and distance in your relationship.

In summary, as you meet the needs of your child who is adopted, you will help build attachment with your child. Attachment will help facilitate the healing of your child. In addition, you want to create patterns in your child's life that communicate the value of their voice. Even when chaos erupts, try to figure out how you can help meet your child's needs. It's about connection, especially when chaos abounds!

It's about one caring adult! Show me a child who is not connected, and I will show you a child with behavioral problems.

> **Lessons Learned**
>
> 1. In the moment of chaos, show support and empathy and use few words.
> 2. Provide reflective, supportive comments to help move toward connection.
> 3. Find special opportunities to connect with your child. In our family, we have "special treats" where I take my son or daughter out individually to their favorite restaurant at least once a month for connection, building memories, and bonding.
> 4. Maintain your sense of humor and be playful in your interactions.
> 5. Practice a 4 to 1 praise-to-correction ratio. When you need to correct your child, make sure you use at least four more praises before having to make another correction. Try to use the sandwich technique when possible. In this technique, you begin with a praise, provide the correction, and immediately follow it up with another praise.

References

Archer, C., & Gordon, C. (2013). *Reparenting the Child Who Hurts: A Guide to Healing Developmental Trauma and Attachments*. Jessica Kingsley Publishers.

Field, T., Kilmer, T., Hernanandez-Reif, M., & Burman, I. (1996). Preschool Children's Sleep and Wake Behavior: Effects of Massage Therapy. *Early Child Dev Care*. 120, 39–44.

Golding, K.S., & Hughes, D.A. (2012). *Creating Loving Attachments: Parenting With PACE to Nurture Confidence and Security in the Troubled Child*. Jessica Kingsley Publishers.

Hart, S., Field, T., Hernandez-Reif, M., & Lundy, B. (1998). *Preschooler's Cognitive Performance Improves Following Message*. Early Child Dev Care. 143, 59–64.

Hughes, D.A., & Baylin, J. (2012). *Brain-Based Parenting: The Neuroscience of Caregiving for Healthy Attachment*. W.W. Norton & Company.

Li, Q., Zhao, W., & Kendrick, K. (2022). Affective Touch in the Context of Development, Oxytocin Signaling, With Autism. *Front Psychol.* 13.

Perry, B.P., & Winphrey, O. (2021). *What Happened to You? Conversations on Trauma, Resilience, and Healing*. Macmillan.

Purvis, K.B., Cross, D.R., Dansereau, D.F., & Parris, S.R. (2013). Trust Based Relationship Intervention (TBRI®): A Systematic Approach to Complex Developmental Trauma. *Child Youth Serv.* 34 (4), 360–384. https://doi.org/10.1080/0145935X.2013.859906

Purvis, K.B., Cross, D.R., & Sunshine, W.L. (2007). *The Connected Child*. McGraw Hill.

Roth, I. (2010). *The Autism Spectrum in the 21st Century. Exploring Psychology, Biology, and Practice*. Jessica Kingsley Publishers.

Siegel, D., & Bryson, T.P. (2019). *The Yes Brain: How to Cultivate Courage, Curiosity, and Resilience in Your Child*. Bentham.

Correcting Your Child's Conduct

7

If your goal is to simply change the behavior of your foster/adoptive child, you will likely end up as a defeated foster/adoptive parent. However, if your primary goal is to how to connect with your child during a chaotic situation, you will find that your child will be in a better environment to learn new behavioral skills and coping strategies that will last a lifetime.

Trust-Based Relational Intervention (TBRI®) emphasized empowering, connecting, and correcting principles. In this chapter, I want to outline my personal suggestions for you to be able to better connect with your child. TBRI® and the science of behavioral research that stems from years of empirical support emphasize the need to balance nurture and structure. If you are all about nurture but you do not have structure, you will end up with a loved child who may become spoiled and entitled. However, if you emphasize obedience, structure, and rules without nurture, you will likely see a rebellious child when they get older. Therefore, it is important to have a balanced approach to trauma-informed parenting.

Purvis *et al.* (2013) outline that the goal of correction can only occur under the umbrella of connection and empowerment. Too often than not, I see parents (including myself) who forget about the goal of connection when correcting behaviors. Our own emotions and frustrations seem to bubble up, and we lose sight of connecting with our own children in the midst of correcting them.

Often, kids with trauma history get stuck in old patterns of behavior, and they do not have the skills to turn it around. TBRI® and applied behavior analysis (ABA) encourage parents to practice the skills they want to teach. The "Re-do" can be a positive approach to parenting in which you help the child to learn a better response (Purvis *et al.*, 2007, pp. 97–98). It is positive because you praise the positive rather than punish the negative behavior as well. Also, doing the "re-do" is a great opportunity to

DOI: 10.4324/9781003601081-10

practice growth and development and praise and reinforce the behavior you want to see. After a "re-do", your child will hopefully feel good about practicing the alternative way to meet the same need. It takes a lot of repetition to help teach a child how to engage in more appropriate, socially significant behaviors.

When your foster/adoptive child lashes out with words or behaviors that seem to push you away, remember that your initial response can be empathy with the goal of connection. As hard as it may be, here is my advice to you. Speak in a calm and relaxed voice (rather than a tense voice). Respond by saying something like:

- "I see that you really hate me".
- "I understand you wish I would not adopt you".
- "I see that you are really upset at me and that make sense. I am here for you, and if you want to share more, I am here to listen to your hurt and pain".

You eventually will need to have a firm but loving discussion with your child and help teach your child how to communicate their needs in a respectful manner when upset; however, this is best done with a regulated child who is calm and in their prefrontal lobe (the relaxed and thinking part of the brain). I am confident you will not have a meaningful conversation when your child is angry or fearful as their limbic part of their brain short circuits the prefrontal lobe.

It is important to slow down your rhythm and sincerely attempt to hear more of your child's hurt or frustration, even when they lash out at you.

After your foster/adoptive child shares their frustration with you and is calm and alert, you can then do a "re-do". You may say something like, perhaps, instead of saying, "I hate you". You could have said, "I am really mad at you". If you try to lecture your child when they are dysregulated, you will likely keep them in the flight/fight system in their brain (the limbic system) where they will not be capable of reasoning at the moment.

Coregulation is the key. Coregulation occurs as you seek to provide a calm and reassuring presence when your child is in a heightened state of emotional instability. Your calm, relaxed, and reassuring demeanor can spread to your child to help them become in a relaxed state. When you remain calm and relaxed and speak with a gentle tone, you will help your child move from the limbic system to their prefrontal lobe of their brain. It may mean that you feel like a punching bag at the moment, but your child's anger, frustration, and hurt will eventually subside after they feel heard. Furthermore, they will be more likely to listen to you when they know they are heard.

Regulated people regulate people. Focus on helping your child to regulate first, then you can focus on their behavior!

As you support your children to help them move from the dysregulated limbic system to the regulated frontal lobe of their brain, you will then have the best environment so you can discuss and address behavioral concerns.

Depending on the unique situation, you may consider helping your child practice some coping strategies to release some of their tension in their bodies. Perhaps, you can encourage your child to push their hands against a wall. I have found that many youths who experience a lot of anger can find it helpful to tense their entire body and gradually blow out all their frustrations with an exhale. When my son was younger, he used to always ask for an "Anaconda squeeze". I would wrap my arms around him and squeeze his body. When I would do this, you could literally see the tension in his body become more relaxed. The key is to try to find some type of coping mechanism that your child may find to release their frustration at the first sign of distress.

It is important to understand that children are not able to regulate and calm themselves down unless they have had a rich history of their needs being met by a stable caregiver. When this occurs, a child learns to coregulate with an adult. Finally, when a child learns how to coregulate, he/she can then eventually learn how to self-regulate a child. One of the worst things we can do for a child with a trauma history (especially a history of neglect) is to send them away to calm down by themselves if they do not have the tools to calm down by themselves. Sometimes, a child may need to take space, but we also want to remind the child that you are available if need be.

Dr. Dan Siegel, a pioneer in childhood trauma, developed a concept called the "Window of tolerance". The window of tolerance is the amount of change or frustration that one can experience before becoming dysregulated. On one end of the window is chaos. Chaos can be described as a volcano of emotions and reactivity. On the other side of the window is flexibility and adaptability (Siegel, 2020). Children with trauma histories likely have a very small window of tolerance. In other words, they will not be able to tolerate too much before experiencing a meltdown. Many children with trauma histories, especially those with a rich history of neglect, are not used to having their needs met by comforting adults. As a result, their window of tolerance becomes very small. Trauma-informed foster parents (TIFPs) seek to become aware of their child's window of tolerance and seek to help coregulate their child at the first sign of dysregulation. The good news is that the size of the window of tolerance can be shifted or widened as we help build new coping strategies and adjust how we respond to our children when your child shows signs of dysregulation.

The key is to connect in the moment of chaos.

Connection without Correction will likely backfire!

We know from brain research that there is something called the sensory neural motor loop…If I do the thing I heard about, I have a body memory for it. When a child does the wrong thing, they have a memory for the wrong thing… We want our child to have the motor memory for doing the right thing…. The path to the negative behavior might be an eight-lane freeway, and the path to the behavior you may want might be a little machete chopped jungle vine bridge somewhere in the dense forest. Every time my child practices with me (an action- based practice), they chop away some more vine, and this little jungle path may become a freeway. (Wilson et al., 2021)

I want to focus on giving my child more opportunities to engage in the right behavior and have a body memory for that. That is why the "Re-do" is so effective.

I do not play golf anymore, but I used to golf. I love the concept of the mulligan, and I tend to use them a lot. A mulligan means that you hit the ball of course, and you pretend it did not occur. You don't beat yourself up, you simply do a re-do, to try to make it better.

Let's give lots of mulligans to our foster/adoptive children.

Purvis et al. (2007) suggests parents can ask 'Are you asking or telling?' as a playful way to respond when your child makes a demand Let's provide an example this approach with a re-do:

CHILD	"Give me water!"
PARENT	"Oh, are you asking or telling?"
CHILD	"I am asking!"
PARENT	"Can you ask me more politely?" (The Re-Do)
CHILD	"Can I please have some water?"
PARENT	"Absolutely, I am on it!"

Children with trauma histories may naturally feel they are a "bad" child or have shame when redirecting their behavior. That is why it is important for TIFPs to make sure your child knows that you love them, accept them no matter what! Sometimes, you may not like their behavior, but you will always love them!

Purvis *et al.* (2013, p. 374) outline the following four levels of response when correcting behavior:

- Playful engagement
- Structured engagement
- Calming engagement
- Protective engagement

Purvis *et al.* (2013) state that using *playful engagement* with your child as a primary technique for low-level behaviors such as disrespect. For example, if your child demands to give you water, you can respond, "Hey there, little monkey, are you asking or telling? This playful interaction can be followed up with a re-do" (Purvis *et al.*, 2013, p. 374). We use *structured engagement* if level one does not work. In this level, you should provide a few choices to help your child make a better decision. *Calming engagement* occurs if structured engagement does not work. In this stage, you can prompt your child to use a calming strategy or redirect your child to take space. If this does not work, the last stage is *protective engagement* where the primary goal is to maintain safety for your child due to the risk of the child or someone else being harmed. Once your child is regulated and safe, you move back to playful engagement and work toward a redo at that point (Purvis *et al.*, 2013, p. 374).

Sometimes, we as foster parents react too strongly to misbehavior with a level of engagement that could have been redirected in a more playful manner. Have you ever seen a parent who scolds their child for doing a childish behavior such as accidentally spilling the milk? It can happen to the best of us.

Lessons Learned

1. Whenever possible, aim for connection, even in your correction.
2. If you are not calm yourself, take a personal timeout before correcting your child. It is perfectly fine to wait a little while after the situation resolves to provide the correction. However, it is important for you to be calm and regulate yourself as you are seeking to correct your child.
3. Your response to your child's maladaptive behavior will either assist and support your child by helping to build them up or possibly re-traumatize your child by using harsh or abrasive parenting practices.
4. Stop just trying to focus on changing your child's behavior. First, view your child as a person who needs to connect with you. Remember that your child needs to learn more skills. Hopefully, this will lead you to be more playful and empathetic in your response.
5. The "Re-do" can be a powerful tool to help teach your child more appropriate response. When possible, do the "re-do" in a playful manner.

References

Purvis, K.B., Cross, D.R., Dansereau, D.F., & Parris, S.R. (2013). Trust Based Relationship Intervention (TBRI®): A Systematic Approach to Complex Developmental Trauma. *Child Youth Serv.* 34 (4), 360–384. https://doi.org/10.1080/0145935X.2013.859906

Purvis, K.B., Cross, D.R., & Sunshine, W.L. (2007). *The Connected Child*. McGraw Hill.

Siegel, D. (2020). *The Developing Mind: How Relationships and the Brain Interact to Shape Who We Are*. Guilford Press.

Wilson, J.D., Ottinger, T., & Ottinger, M. (2021). A Deep Dive into Dr. Karyn Purvis' IDEAL Response (Episode 26) [Audio podcast episode]. In *Empowered to Connect*. https://empowered-to-connect-podcast.castos.com/?search=IDEAL

Section III

Behavior Change for Trauma-Informed Foster Parenting

In this section, we will look at behavior change strategies that are effective for children with trauma histories. However, before we jump in, it is important to understand the concept of the function of behavior. When looking at behaviors associated with trauma, it is important to remember that all behavior serves a function. All behaviors including meltdowns, defiance, aggression, lying, and stealing serve a purpose. You may not understand why your child may engage in certain behaviors and there may not be any observable trigger, but I promise you these behaviors likely just do not just pop up willy-nilly. In fact, your child's first language was their behavior. Over the years, your child has learned how to communicate through their behaviors. There is likely an environmental cause for your child's behavior. Trauma-informed foster and adoptive parents try to be aware of the function or cause of behavior before addressing the behavior. Once we determine the function of the behavior, Trauma-informed foster parents (TIFPs) seek to determine new skills and new behaviors to replace the maladaptive behaviors that may serve the same function. You may refer to your child's behavior as "challenging" or "problematic"; however, their behavior likely is not "challenging" or "problematic to them", it is only challenging or problematic to us as their foster/adoptive parents. Your child's behaviors are functional for your child. It may take a bit of detective work on your part, but it is critical for you to always consider the purposes or function that your child's behavior may serve. If you think about, your child's behavior makes sense! It likely meets a need or serves as a form of communication. All behavior serves a purpose! For example, your child's behavior may serve and meet a need to gain something such as a sense of safety when their nervous system may be all out of whack or may serve a function to escape a difficult feeling they may be experiencing.

DOI: 10.4324/9781003601081-11

There are four main functions of behavior also known as S.E.A.T: **S**ensory, **E**scape, **A**ttention, **T**angible

Sensory

The sensory function means that a child's behavior is reinforcing in itself (without the behavior of another person). An example of a sensory function would be if I were to rub my arm to receive the sensory tactile stimulation of comfort. Another example of a sensory function would be if I were to smell a flower to gain the pleasure of the smell. Or perhaps, a person may talk out loud to stay focused.

Escape

Often, children will engage in a particular behavior to escape a nonpreferred task or an unpleasant feeling. If a young child cries when having a soiled diaper, it hopefully will result in the uncomfortable feeling of the soiled diaper once the diaper is removed. In this case, the child learns that when they cry, they can escape the uncomfortable sensation of a soiled diaper. A child may have a temper tantrum to escape doing a nonpreferred chore as well.

Attention

Children with trauma histories often crave attention. They want to be noticed. Sometimes, children learn that they can get attention (even if it is negative attention) when they engage in certain behaviors. If we know a maladaptive behavior has a function of attention (such as a tantrum), our goal will be to help teach our child how to gain our attention in a more appropriate manner. This would be known as the attention function. Behavior can be maintained by both positive and negative attention.

One of my children used to try to gain attention in his classroom by falling on the ground and rolling around like a fish out of water when they were in the 4th grade. Therefore, I got a joke book for my child and tried to give my child a new way to gain attention from their peers.

Tangible

This is also known as the "Access" function. When a child engages in a behavior to gain access to a tangible or intangible item. For example, a young boy may cry when going into a candy store, so his parents provide him with candy. Well, certainly, he stops crying, but he gets his candy! In this example, the function of his crying behavior is to gain access to candy. If we know a child's behavior has a function of access, we will want to help teach a new skill to this boy so he can learn to access the candy by asking for it (rather than crying).

Unfortunately, childhood trauma can affect a child's ability to regulate their nervous system, and this may result in all kinds of emotional dysregulation and outbursts. The term regulation basically infers that your child is not in a heightened state of fear as he/she is calm and alert. A child who is dysregulated likely is in a state of fear, anger, or heightened emotional reactivity and will likely become easily triggered by environmental stimuli.

Replacement Behaviors and Teaching Strategies

8

Trauma-informed foster parents seek to shift the way they view their child's maladaptive behavioral patterns – the shift from a point of frustration and defeat as a parent to a wonderful opportunity to teach new skills and replacement behaviors.

Before looking at effective behavioral strategies of behavior change let's look at strategies that are ineffective for behavior change. Traditional parenting practices likely will not work for behavior change for a child with a history of trauma. If you rely upon these strategies, you likely will feel defeated as a foster parent. I must confess that I am not the best model at times, and I have resorted to some of these parenting traps at times. Parenting a child with trauma is not easy.

"Reminders, warnings, lecture, threat, and bribes fall under a category I refer to as 'brain sharing'. Parents are doing the thinking for their youngers and the child is happily allowing the scenario to continue" (James, 2019, p.107).

These types of behavior strategies along with punishment strategies (to be discussed in Chapter 11) are some of the least effective strategies for behavior change, yet we as foster and adoptive parents all engage in these traps at times.

Reminders

Both of my children have struggled at times with self-management of their own behaviors. If you have a child with attention-deficit hyperactivity disorder (ADHD), you will know how difficult it can be to

DOI: 10.4324/9781003601081-12

help a child with organization. Often, I have relied upon reminders with my kids,

- "Don't forget to brush your teeth before you go to bed".
- "Don't forget to put your homework in your backpack".
- "Please put the dishes in the dishwasher".
- "When you go to the bathroom, don't forget to put the toilet seat down".
- "Don't forget to close the door while you use the bathroom!".

The problem with reminders is that our kiddos never really learn to think for themselves. They then will rely to rely upon the reminders. Here is what happens in what I refer to as the "Reminder Cycle":

1. Your child does not have a need to put the effort into thinking for himself, and child does not engage in expected task.
2. Child waits for reminder.
3. Parent reminds child.
4. Child engages in the behavior.
5. Repeat! (In fact, your child may be quite content in allowing this pattern to continue.)

The two solutions to stopping the cycle are to allow natural consequences to take in effect (response strategy which will be discussed in Chapter 9) and to teach self-management skills to your child (teaching strategy/replacement behaviors). Here is a good example of how I used natural consequences for one of my children when we were caught up in the "reminder cycle". I was getting frustrated with my child because my child would always forget to wash the dishes and put them in the dishwasher when they were through. I constantly reminded my child to do it. Unfortunately, my child became dependent upon my reminders, so I decided I needed to allow the natural consequences to do the teaching. I let the dishes pile up in the corner, and they did not do so until sometimes there were no plates left. When my child was hungry and had no plate, my child would eventually clean them off. At times, when my child asked for me to cook them some food, I would say something like, "I would love to cook your food, but, unfortunately, am unable to do that because of all these dishes". Well, this approach did take a bit of work, but I started to see improvement in my child remembering this simple chore without my reminders (at least most of the time).

The second way to get out of the reminder cycle is to teach self-management skills. For example, you can help your child learn how to use their own cell phone to give themselves reminders. It would be much better for you to assist your child in setting up a reminder on their cell phone the night before to take out trash than you to remind your child. Everyone is happier. Your child will be elated that you are not nagging and reminding, and you will be thrilled that you do not have to always keep tabs on your child as much. Problem solved!

Threats

- "If you don't take the trash out, you are going to lose your cell phone for 3 hours!"
- "If you don't pick up those toys, I am never going buy you toys again!"

Threats are problematic because they can be effective at the moment. In other words, it can cause a child to stop what they are doing and listen to you, but it comes at a cost. Guess what, if you always threaten your child, your child may learn to not listen to you unless you threaten them. That is a problem. In addition, often, parents do not always follow through with their threats, so our foster/adoptive children will come to not trust us. In addition, threats tend to be more of an authoritarian type of parenting. Children with trauma will certainly try to rebel against authoritative parents and will create more distance between you and your child. That is another problem! In addition, threats are often combined with other ineffective strategies such as yelling and signs of frustration. This may inadvertently create a mindset for your foster or adoptive child that "I am a bad kid".

If you want to build trust with your child, it is important for you to always follow through with what you say. Therefore, you need to be very careful what you say! Most foster/adoptive children with trauma histories have a history of broken trust. They are used to having adults who struggle with meeting their needs and expectations. That is why you need to be very careful with the words you use as well as your tone and nonverbals in the process.

Bribes

A bribe occurs when we tell a child your child that you will give them a positive reward while they are engaging in a maladaptive behavior For example:

- "If you stop pouting, I will take you to get ice cream".
- Saying to a child who is actively refusing to go to school, "If you just go to school today, I will buy you a toy after school".

The problem with bribes is that your child will learn that they get a positive outcome if they persist in engaging in maladaptive behavior. They learn that if they continue protesting, they will eventually be able to get a positive outcome out of it.

Nagging and Lectures

- "How many times have I told you, Stop chewing with your mouth open!"
- "is so important for you to complete your homework and get good grades. I know you can do better. You are not trying your hardest. If you just try harder, I know you can do it!"

Nagging runs the risk of reinforcing a self-belief that your child is incompetent. It certainly can break the self-confidence of our kids. Children with trauma histories already have fragile self-confidence, so our nagging and lectures can be like low blows punches in their gut! Also, the more we nag, the more our kids will tune us out. They simply will shut down to avoid the uncomfortable feeling of lectures and nags. Finally, nagging emphasizes the negative rather than positive. It is much better to reinforce and build up the positive behavior than nag the negative behaviors. Here's my best advice for you: if you can't say in a few sentences, then it is probably better left unsaid!

Why do we as parents nag and lecture all the time? For me, sometimes, I have a false belief that I solely am responsible for my child's behavior. This is a lot of pressure for me, and this leads me to try harder to convince my child to change their behavior. When my goal becomes changing their behavior, I tend to nag and lecture! Ahh, this is so messed up, and yet I still can do it. As a psychologist, I have asked hundreds of children if their parents nag them. I have yet to find a child/youth who tells me that their parents don't nag. If you have a child that says you don't nag, please let me know as I really want to meet you and learn from you!

Many of us were always taught to focus on changing the behavior, rather than looking at the need (the "why") behind the behavior first. The police officer's approach to managing behavior is constantly being on the lookout to see when they mess up and impose a fine (a consequence) when they do.

When you are focused on the police officer approach to changing behavior, you will be more likely to miss the opportunity to teach a skill and meet the need behind the behavior.

In addition, you will always be frustrated and feel behind the curve if you are constantly looking at changing the behaviors as there will always be more behaviors that need to be addressed and changed in your child. Also, it is a much better approach to teach new skills and look at changing the contingencies in the environment that evoke and maintain the behavior.

When your child engages in maladaptive behavior, consider this an opportunity to teach a new skill. It is an opportunity to support growth and development, rather than an opportunity to punish a behavior. Think of misbehavior as an opportunity for your child to learn a new skill.

The Kazdin Method is a notable behavioral method for teaching new behaviors to your foster/adoptive child (Kazdin, 2008). The basic premise is that you come up with the positive opposite of the maladaptive behavior and find ways to reinforce the positive opposite. Therefore, you reinforce the replacement behavior. For example, the positive opposite of leaving clothes on the floor of their room is placing the clothes in the hamper. The positive opposite of procrastinating homework is sitting quietly doing their homework. Kazdin (2008) encourages parents to have "reinforced practice". Kazdin outlines that children need to have lots of opportunities to practice the positive opposite, so they perform the behavior. The main premise is that you work on one behavior at a time. You find the replacement behavior for the maladaptive behavior and your role as a parent is to help teach and encourage your child how to use that behavior. You are not punishing the behavior you do not want to see; in contrast, you are reinforcing the behavior you want to see (Kazdin, 2008).

Although there are not any documented research studies for this specific approach, I have used the principles of the Kazdin Method for my own adoptive children. In addition, I have seen the effectiveness of the Kazdin Method for a countless number of families and children I work with for helping to teach new skills to children with a history of trauma and oppositional behaviors.

The "re-do" is a great opportunity to practice a more adaptive skill after they engage in the maladaptive behavior. A role play is providing a hypothetical situation in which the child either acts out the behavior or identifies the positive opposite/replacement behavior can be a fun strategy to use with your child as well. The natural opportunity occurs when I reinforce my child if they independently engage in the replacement behavior.

I work one behavior at a time. The way I have used this approach is to give 1 point for a role play, 1 point for a redo, and 2 points for natural opportunities to practice the behavior we want to see. Once my children get 10 points, they can cash the points in for $10. I have used this as an opportunity for my kids to learn the value of money as well. For example, if my son wants a pair of VANS shoes that cost $55, I agree to pay $25 for a pair of shoes, and he will have to use his own money to pay for anything more than $25. This creates a greater reason and need to earn points/ money.

Now, there can be a problem with rewards with children with trauma histories. Sometimes, it can be anxiety-provoking for a child who is trying to earn a reward. In addition, you do not want to set up a situation where your child does not engage in behaviors unless they have a reward. Therefore, it is important to use other strategies to maintain behavior with natural consequences, as compared to only relying upon rewards. Children need to learn how to engage in certain behaviors because of natural reinforcement. However, sometimes, it is needed to provide our foster/adoptive children with extrinsic motivation of a reward to get to behavior change. Sometimes, you can start off with a reward to reinforce the behavior to get to intrinsic motivation. Once a child learns how to engage in the appropriate behavior, you then fade the reward (extrinsic motivation) to the natural consequence to help work toward intrinsic motivation. However, it is important to fade out the reward to the natural consequence sooner than later. All in all, rewards should not be your primary tool to help motivate your child to changed behavior.

Here are a few behaviors that I addressed with my own children from the principles of the Kazdin Method:

Maladaptive behavior: Grabbing the remote from the other person.
Behavior to reinforce: Asking nicely for the remote.

Maladaptive behavior: Profanity.
Behavior to reinforce: Saying a substitute word such as "Rats".

It is best to come up with a reward in which the only way to gain access to the reward is by earning points. For example, perhaps, the reward is that you will take your son/daughter to Chucky Cheese if they get a certain number of points. The key is that you want to make sure that is the only way to go to Chucky Cheese. In addition, try to get the input from your son/daughter on what they would like to have as their reward, so they are more motivated to get points. When a child is excited for what they are working toward, they will be more willing to practice the skill.

The question some parents ask is how they respond if the child never engages in the behavior. If this occurs, it is a good idea to increase the role plays with him. This gives your child more opportunities to practice the skill that they have not yet learned to do through natural opportunities. Now, it is your turn, you try this effective approach!

Teaching new skills is about using positive reinforcement to reinforce the behaviors you want to see. In addition, trauma-informed foster and adoptive parents tend to do whatever is possible to help their children feel safe. Finding ways to catch your child being good and reinforce the behavior you want them to engage in is a good strategy to help support appropriate behaviors for your child. I encourage foster parents just to go out of their way to notice their child. Take a "snapshot" moment of observing your child and comment upon what they are doing, even in a neutral manner. For example, you can say, "I see you watching television, I hope you are enjoying it!". This is a good way to highlight that you simply are aware of your child. This also can help to provide a sense of felt safety to your child.

Lessons Learned

1. Don't expect that your child will know what to do to stop their maladaptive behavioral patterns. You can give your child lots of practice opportunities and "re-do's" to help your child learn new skills of responding in a more adaptive manner.
2. Our role as a parent is to be more of a coach and teacher rather than a police officer who seeks to catch our child making a bad choice. Catch them being good! And repeat!
3. When you observe a behavior that you do not observe in your child, try to come up with the behavior you want to see instead that meets the same need/function. Find ways to teach and reinforce the behavior you want to see rather than lecture, nag, or remind your child of the behaviors you do not wish to see.

References

Kazdin, A.E. (2008). *The Kazdin Method for Parenting the Defiant Child*. Houlton Mifflin.
James, A. (2019). *The Science of Parenting Adopted Children*. Jessica Kingsley Publishing.

Relying on Proactive Strategies

9

> Trauma-informed foster parents are proactive in always trying to predict when their child or teen may become frustrated of overwhelmed and seeks to help prepare their child for what is to come; on the other hand, if you tend to be reactive after the chaos erupts, you will likely be in a constant state of repair.

There is well-documented research about the effectiveness of applied behavior analysis (ABA) for behavior change. There are countless studies that show ABA is effective for teaching new skills and reducing maladaptive behavior. ABA is a science that focuses on using principles of behavior change such as positive reinforcement, shaping, chain, and differential reinforcement to help teach new skills and improve socially significant behaviors. The National Autism Center (NAC) re-reviewed well over 200 articles between 2007 and 2012 and evaluated ABA as being evidence-based with established support (NAC, 2015).

In 1999, the Surgeon's General Report highlighted there are 30 years of research that demonstrate "the efficacy of applied behavioral methods in reducing inappropriate behavior and in increasing prosocial communications, learning, and appropriate social behavior". Since this report in the last 20 years, there have been countless research studies and single-subject designs that continue to support these findings.

The principles of behavior change rooted in ABA that can help your foster/adoptive child. We learn from behavioral research and the field of ABA that there are environmental changes that can be made to help change behavior. There are three environmental changes that can be made to change behavior: proactive strategies, response strategies, and teaching strategies (Figure 9.1).

DOI: 10.4324/9781003601081-13

WAYS TO CHANGE BEHAVIOR

Antecedent	Behavior	Consequence
⬇	⬇	⬇
Proactive Strategies	**Teaching Strategies**	**Responding Strategies**
Choose the way you respond BEFORE the behavior occurs	Teach a new skill	Choose the way you respond AFTER the behavior occurs

Figure 9.1 Ways to Change Behavior

Proactive strategies are things you do before the behavior occurs to prevent the behavior from occurring. This is so important to understand when coming to managing the disruptive behavior of your children.

Response strategies are strategies that parents/caretakers can do after a behavior occurs. Some use the term reactive strategies, but I prefer to use the term "response strategies" as response tends to portray a more thoughtful and intentional response to behaviors.

Many foster/adoptive parents tend to falsely view response strategies as the only way to change behavior. This is not true. The best way to change behavior is by reinforcing the behavior you want to see (i.e., teaching strategies).

Teaching strategies are specific things you do as a foster/adoptive parent/caretaker to help your child learn new skills. When learned, these new skills will help your child with their maladaptive behaviors. These strategies must serve the same function as the maladaptive behavior.

The following six proactive strategies of choice making, priming, Premack principle, behavioral momentum, noncontingent attention (NCA), and noncontingent escape (NCE) have solid behavioral research of efficacy.

The Power of Choice

A child with a trauma history may have learned a type of survival instinct to want to be in control. Your child may be operating out of fear – fear of abandonment, fear of abuse, fear of going hungry. As a result, they learn that it is much safer to not depend upon others and try to control their environment. Really, it makes sense if you think about it. I need to remain in control at all costs!

The more "controlling" a child is, the more choices you need to provide!

Choices may provide an excellent way to help your child feel like he/she has some sense of control. Providing choices can be a great proactive strategy to help reduce noncompliance. I have found that choices were especially effective for my own children. When they were younger, I would give them choices throughout the day.

- Do you want to eat with the blue plate or the red plate?
- Do you want to have two pillows or three pillows on your bed?
- Do you want me to tuck you in or do you want to tuck yourself in?
- Do you want to eat corn or green beans for dinner?
- Would you like to work on your math or spelling first?

By providing lots of opportunities to make choices, it helps to empower your child and meet their need to find control and balance in their own life.

In addition, choices can be a great way to get your child who tends to be defiant to do something. Instead of saying, "Go clean your room now". You can say, "Do you want to clean your room before or after dinner?" This may help your child greatly.

Have you ever provided a negative consequence to your child and immediately got a response of "That's not fair! You are so mean!"? If you do have to put a negative consequence to a behavior (which should not be your "go to" strategy unless other reinforcement-based behavioral strategies have been used first), it may be good for you to provide choice in the process. For example, you can say, "would you prefer to write a letter to you sister to apologize for your behavior or would you prefer to write 'Be respectful when mad' fifty times on a piece of paper?"

In providing choices, a trauma-informed foster parent (TIFP) seeks to allow natural consequences to do the teaching when possible. Dr. Bruce Perry highlighted, "To develop a self, one must exercise choice and learn from the consequences of those choices; if the only thing you are taught is to comply, you have little way of knowing what you like and want" (Perry, 2017). Indeed, children can only learn responsibility when they fail, and most failures involve choices.

There is a lot of empirical, behavioral-based research from the field of ABA that shows child choice increases a child's motivation to learn. By offering choice to your child, it will not only increase their motivation to grow and learn, but it will also likely help to facilitate your child's development.

One intervention derived from the principles of ABA was developed by Robert and Lynn Koegel. This intervention called Pivotal Response Training focuses on the use of child choice to increase motivation and learning. Koegel and Koegel determined "child choice" was considered a "pivotal behavior". Pivotal behaviors are behaviors that once learned will result in an increase in other behaviors (Koegel *et al.*, 1999).

This evidence-based behavioral approach involves helping children learn by using child choice and shared control. By following the child's lead, the teacher can help the child by increasing their motivation to learn. At the same time, it can help to reduce maladaptive behaviors associated with learning because the child is more involved in the learning process with their choice (Koegel *et al.*, 1988; Stahmer, 1995).

Studies in psychology have linked child choice to intrinsic motivation. However, it was also discovered that one can have choice overload if provided too many choices. (Iyengar & Lepper, 1999). Therefore, it may be best to offer simple and few choices when possible.

The Power of Priming

Priming is a behavioral intervention that is used to help individuals transition for an upcoming event or activity. The basic premise is to use a short, concise statement about the behavior you expect to see. For example, if your child is swimming in the pool, you can say, "We are going to get out in 10 more minutes". You can also give a 5-minute warning or a 1-minute warning as well. This simple behavioral tool has been shown to be quite effective at helping to reduce noncompliance and outbursts associated with transitions for children (Sevin *et al.*, 2015).

One strategy I use with my own children in priming is to try to get ownership of a plan before it happens. For example, let's say I anticipate that my child will not want to go on an errand with me as they are in the middle of watching a television show. I may say to them, "I know this television show is important to you, but I also need to go buy groceries. I was going to go now to the store, but how about we wait until after the show and then go, sound good?" By saying "sound good?", I am trying to create ownership in the plan with my child to help create the greater possibility of a smooth transition.

The Power of the Premack Principle

The main idea of the Premack principle is that you allow one behavior to reinforce another behavior. Specifically, the lower probability behavior is reinforced by the more desirable higher probability behavior. The lower probability behavior is the behavior that is less likely to occur. It is also known as "Grandma's rule" (Herrod *et al.*, 2023). Some people think of it as a "first, then" contingency if the "then" is the more preferred activity as compared to the "first".

Here are some examples of the Premack principle:

- "Eat our vegetables first (lower probability behavior), then you get dessert (higher probability behavior)". The dessert serves as a reinforcer and motivation for eating vegetables".
- "Do your homework first (lower probability behavior), then you get to play video games (higher probability behavior)". The video games serve as a reinforcer for doing their homework. Have you ever tried to get your son/daughter to do homework when they have been playing video games? Yeah, I know. That doesn't work very well because the environmental contingencies are a bit whacky!

The Power of the Paradox

If your child tends to do the opposite of what you ask, the power of the paradox may help! Sometimes, our kids will seek to remain in control, even if you ask them to do something they want. The power of the paradox is to basically prescribe the symptom you expect to see. If your child normally has a tantrum when you ask them to clean their room, you can say, "Okay, in about 5 minutes, I would like you to clean your room. Please be sure to have a tantrum when you do so!" If you do this, be sure to secretly video your child's response to this. You may get a blank stare or a "Wait, What did you just say?" type of response. Sometimes, such a paradox intervention may be the trick to throw your child off a bit in a direction of greater compliance.

The Power of Behavioral Momentum

Behavioral momentum is another behavioral strategy that can be used to help with defiance. It has been shown by behavioral research/ABA that an individual will increase his/her compliance when the rate of responding for easy tasks is introduced. In other words, individuals tend to keep doing what they start to do with momentum; therefore, if you jump-start a defiant child with an easy request, they will likely continue what they started (i.e., you get the child on a roll). Once you get a child to comply with something easy (high-probability request), you then will find it is easier to get your child to do something that is a bigger, harder request (low-probability request). The way this works is you get your child to do several easy tasks that are considered high-probability requests at a rapid-fire, and then you ask them to do a less desirable task. You then end on the low-probability request (Mace *et al.*, 1988; DeLeon *et al.*, 2013). For example, let's say your child hates to clean their room. You could try this approach by giving the following requests in a quick fashion!

- "Give me high five" (higher probability behavior)
- "Race me upstairs" (high-probability behavior)
- "Pick up this one toy" (high-probability behavior)
- "Give me another high five" (high-probability behavior)
- "Put your shirt in the dirty laundry" (high-probability behavior)
- "Now, finish picking up your room" (lower probability behavior)

The idea is that you create behavioral momentum, so it increases the possibility that they will complete the task.

The Power of Noncontingent Reinforcement (NCR)

NCR is a behavioral procedure in which you provide attention at regular intervals (regardless of behavior). NCR can be used when you know that a particular child is acting out to receive attention. If a child acts out to receive attention, by providing NCA at regular intervals, you create an environment where the child will be less likely to engage in disruptive behavior to gain your attention (Wallace *et al.*, 2012).

Let's say that you know that your child engages in a particular behavior such as gaining attention from the teacher by making disruptive comments. The teacher would then set an interval and would be sure to provide attention to that child at a regular interval (i.e., every 20 minutes). By providing high doses of attention to the student, the student now loses motivation to be disruptive because he/she knows he will be receiving a lot of attention. This would be considered a proactive strategy as you are providing attention ahead of time to reduce the likelihood of the student engaging in attention-seeking disruptive behavior.

The Power of Noncontingent Escape (NCE)

NCE is a similar procedure in which you provide regular intervals of escape from a non-preferred task to reduce the possibility that your foster/child will engage in maladaptive behaviors to escape (Geiger *et al.*, 2010). Let's say, for example, your adopted child engages in a tantrum to escape having to do homework. You can provide a behavioral intervention that you provide escape to your child every 10 minutes when doing their homework. This will reduce the possibility of your foster/adoptive child to engage in a tantrum to remove the stimulus of the homework.

Lessons Learned

1. Proactive strategies to avoid behaviors are often overlooked. However, foster parents will likely find greater success with using proactive strategies to avoid behavior as compared to punishing maladaptive behavior.
2. Providing expectations about upcoming transitions and attempting to get ownership with your child may help reduce the chances of a chaotic transition.
3. Children with trauma histories do better with structure and advance warnings for transitions and change. A TIFP is aware of how change can put their child in a frenzy and seeks to minimize disruptions by using priming whenever possible.
4. Providing choices to your child is a great way to help reduce noncompliance for your child.
5. Try to anticipate how a potential change may cause tension for your child. Show understanding and support for your child's hesitancy.

References

DeLeon, I.G., Gregory, M.K., & St. Peter, C.C. (2013). Recent Developments in Behavioral Intervention Informed by Basic Research. *Int Rev Res Dev Disabil*. 44, 213–244.

Geiger, K.B., Carr, J.E., & Leblanc, L.A. (2010). Function-Based Treatments for Escape-Maintained Problem Behavior: a Treatment-Selection Model for Practicing Behavior Analysts. *Behav Anal Pract*. 3 (1), 22–32. https://doi.org/10.1007/BF03391755

Herrod, J.L., Snyder, S.K., Hart, J.B., Frantz, S.J., & Ayres, K.M. (2023). Applications of the Premack Principle: A Review of the Literature. *Behav Modif*. 47 (1), 219–246. https://doi.org/10.1177/01454455221085249

Iyengar, S.S., & Lepper, M.R. (1999). Rethinking the Value of Choice: A Cultural Perspective on Intrinsic Motivation. *J Personality Social Psychol*, 76(3), 349–366. https://doi.org/10.1037/0022-3514.76.3.349

Koegel, R.L., Schreibman, L., Good, A., Cergnili, L., & Murphy, C. (1988). *How to Teach Pivotal Behaviors to Children with Autism: A Training Manual*. Distributed by ERIC Clearinghouse.

Koegel, L.K., Koegel, R.L., Harrower, J.K., & Carter, C.M. (1999). Pivotal Response Intervention I: Overview of Approach. *J Assoc Pers Sev Handicaps*. 24 (3), 174. https://doi.org/10.2511/rpsd.24.3.174

Mace, F.C., Hock, M.L., Lali, J.S., West, B.J., Belfiore, P., Pinter, E., & Brown, D.K. (1988). Behavioral Momentum in the Treatment of Noncompliance. *J. Appl Beh Anal*. 21 (2), 123–141.

National Autism Center. (2015). *Findings and Conclusions: National Standards Project, Phase 2*. National Autism Center: Randolph, MA.

Perry, B.D. (2017). *The Boy Who Was Raised as a Dog: And Other Stories from a Child Psychiatrist's Notebook*. Basic Book: New York.

Sevin, J.A., Riske, R.D., & Matson, J.L. (2015). A Review of Behavioral Strategies and Support Considerations for Assisting Persons with Difficulties Transitioning from Activity to Activity. *Rev J Autism Dev Disord*. 2, 329–342.

Stahmer, A.C. (1995). Teaching Symbolic Play Skills to Children with Autism Using Pivotal Response Training. *J Autism Dev Disord*. 25(2), 123–141. doi: 10.1007/BF02178500. PMID: 7559281.

United States Surgeon General. (1998). *Mental Health: A Report of the Surgeon General*. United States Surgeon General: Washington, DC.

Wallace, M.D., Iwata, B.A., Hanley, G.P., Thompson, R.H., & Roscoe, E.M. (2012). Noncontingent Reinforcement: a Further Examination of Schedule Effects During Treatment. *J Appl Behav Anal*. 45 (4), 709–719. https://doi.org/10.1901/jaba.2012.45-709

Responding Strategies 10

Trauma-informed foster parents do not have the ability to fix or change our children in foster care. However, they constantly reflect and evaluate how to change their own behavioral response when their child engages in maladaptive behavior patterns. In fact, if their goal is to try to fix their child or change their behaviors, they will likely feel very defeated as parents. On the other hand, if they seek to find ways of changing their own response, they will maintain a greater ownership and control of the situation.

As trauma-informed foster parents (TIFPs), we have all made those parental mistakes by reacting versus responding. There are many interactions with my children that I reacted and wished I could take back. Let's look at the difference between responding and reacting. Reacting comes from the Latin word, "back, perform, to do". In other words, when one reacts, he/she is taking action back at someone (with their behaviors). Reacting occurs when we give a quick response before showing an empathetic, connected approach. On the other hand, the Latin word for "respond" is "back, answer". When one responds, he/she is providing an answer to someone with their words.

Responding is the work of my cerebral cortex, where I am interacting with my child in a deliberate, rational, empathetic, and respectful tone. Reacting occurs when I interact with my child without much deliberation; it is the product of the reactive survival instinct of the amygdala. When there is an argument, you often have two people who are reacting, so that means a double whammy with way too much amygdala for my comfort level.

The first step is to be aware of your own triggers. Recall the times in which you snapped at your adoptive child. Recall situations in which you were not as patient with him/her. Try to identify your feelings at the time. Did you feel confused? Misunderstood? Criticized? Powerless? Embarrassed? Blamed? It is important for you to identify your own

DOI: 10.4324/9781003601081-14

feelings and triggers, so you can move toward responding to the maladaptive behavior of your child rather than reacting to it. When we are not away of our own triggers, we may seek to try to control the situation, which will lead to behaviors such as yelling or losing our own cool that we may later regret.

You can ask yourself the following two questions:

1.   What is going on in me?
2.   What is going on in my child?

When you consider these variables before reacting, it will help you to be better empathize and connect with your child.

Choose Connection and Collaboration as Compared to Control

When our child/teen is upset or mad, this is a wonderful natural opportunity to try to empathize, connect, and seek collaborative solutions. On the other hand, when we seek to control a situation, it likely will end up in a power struggle or a reactive response on our part.

You are not responsible for your child's response. You are only responsible for your own reaction.

When you focus on managing your own reaction, you will naturally avoid seeking to control your child's behavior.

You can shift your focus from "How can I change my child's behavior?" to "How can I manage my own response?"

I have a trigger. When my children cuss at me, I must work hard at responding verses reacting. There have been many occasions in which I ended up raising my voice and saying, "That is not okay!" when my teenager cussed at me in a point of frustration. However, when I do this, I am just providing a fun payoff for my teen as they learn they can "control" my response when they are upset. Sometimes, our teenagers know the buttons to push to get a reaction from us. In a sense, we can begin like their favorite video game as they learn they can "push our buttons" to get a certain reaction from us.

When I was younger, I would never have ever thought about using profanity in the presence of my parents, so it is hard for me to relate. I work hard at trying to show respect to them and other people, so my experiences have made it much easier for me to be triggered by children who constantly use disrespectful works toward their parents.

Let's consider two situations:

Situation One:

PARENT	"Good morning. I need you to get out of bed and get ready for school"
CHILD	"Go away, B—!"
PARENT	"That is not okay. I do not like your language!
CHILD	"Well, I don't like you waking me up!!!
PARENT	"You need to get up now!" (Raising voice)

And yes, this was a situation that has occurred for me. In this situation, my child was reacting and had a survival instinct where their amygdala overrides everything. My child was tired and did not want to get out of bed. This is normal! In addition, I reacted out of my amygdala as well. I did not appreciate my child's language and disrespect and failed to show empathy and connection in the process. I was more concerned about giving his/her child an alternative response before showing empathy. Yes, it was a situation I wish I could have taken back, but the good news is that an apology goes a long way! Empathy and connection first, then problem-solving and repair. After you do these things, you can then help your son/daughter with potential replacement behaviors and alternative responses. I am more likely to have success with my children when they are not hungry or tired and their prefrontal lobe is fully activated. I should have had more sympathy for my child that they were tired and realized that their reactive part of their brain was in full force. I want to be able to help my child by showing empathy first before seeking to correct their behavior. By doing this, I am helping my child transition from their reactive part of their brain (the limbic system) to the thinking/rational part of their brain (frontal cortex).

Situation Two:

PARENT	"Good morning. How did you sleep?"
CHILD	"Go away, fool!"
PARENT	"I hear you. I have had those nights as well. Would you like a few more minutes of sleep?"
CHILD	"Yeah"(!)

A few minutes later....

PARENT	"I know it is tough and you are tired, but it is time to wake up. Would you like some eggs and bacon this morning?
CHILD	"Yes, please"(!)
PARENT	"Good choice, maybe that will help get you going. Let's go ahead and get up and I will go make you breakfast".

In situation #2, the parent did not do the redo immediately. He/she waited until their child was already up and in a better mood to focus for processing his/her behavior and helping him/her to learn the new skill of asking for more sleep time. In addition, the parent provided his/her child with a choice to feel like he/she had some sense of control.

In this situation, the parent was able to "respond" rather than "react". The parent was able to prevent their own amygdala from firing up!

DO NOT RESPOND UNTIL THE ADRENALINE IS GONE.

I used to think that the best time to deal with a situation was right there in the moment. However, if you do this, your response does not gel with what we know about how the brain works. Remember, sometimes, the best solution is to ignore a behavior until the threat has passed, and then process it with your child afterward. We need to wait until our child is calm and regulated to help process their behaviors.

About 15 minutes, later, as your child is eating…

PARENT	You know, when I wake up, I am grumpy too. It sure is hard in the mornings, right?
CHILD	Yeah!

PARENT	Perhaps, in the future, if you are tired, you can ask respectfully for a few more minutes. I think this will help you get up gradually. Can you try that sometime, so I can know to give you a little space"?
CHILD	Sure, I guess.
PARENT	Awesome! Thanks for giving that a shot.

Now, when your child does that in the future, be very intentional about giving him/her what they want (a gradual wake-up). Consequences, signs of disapproval, or lectures will not likely work in this situation. However, a TIFP would know this would likely backfire. Instead, seek to reinforce the behaviors you want to see rather than focus on punishing the behaviors that you do not want to see.

Dr. Bruce Perry is a pioneering neuroscientist in trauma. He outlined "Three R's" of sequential engagement (Regulate, Relate, and Reason) for parents to learn how to respond to their children in a way that helps them to learn, relate, and think (Perry & Winphrey, 2021).

Regulate

In Perry & Winprey (2001), Dr. Perry outlines that the basic need is regulation. The first step of TIFP(ing) is to seek to calm the fear of your child. Regulate, Regulate, Regulate! When a child is in state of fear or high anxiety, our goal as TIFPs should be to work toward regulation first. This is the work of a region of our brain called the diencephalon. This part of the brain acts as a relay station to process the sensory input into our brain as well as to engage the autonomic processes of our body (which regulates involuntary processes such as breathing, heart rate, and blood pressure). It is crucial to help to co-regulate your child by being calm with few words when you observe fear or emotion sinking into your child. This is the point that your regulation can either result in dysregulation or regulation for your child. The key for your response as a trauma-informed adoptive parent is to provide few words and to have a calm, reassuring presence with your child. Your child may need some processing time or a safe place to go. The worst thing you can do in this stage is to express disapproval, lecture, nag, or raise your voice when a child needs to regulate. This will only keep fear alive and keep the fear region of your brain (the amygdala) activated (Perry & Winphrey, 2021).

TIFPs become intently attuned to the regulation needs of their child. The "flight, fight, freeze, and fawn" response is a survival response which

REGULATE	REASON	RELATE
Life threatening or extremely frightening events	A child's experience is the factor that determines whether or not it is traumatic	Can include physical, social, emotional, or spiritual consequences

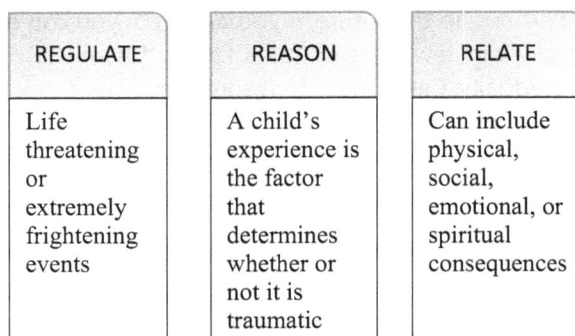

Figure 10.1 The Three R's of Sequential Engagement

is activated when a child interprets the sensory input from becoming too overwhelming or threatening. Just as the sensory input can cause dysregulation; it can also help with regulation. Helping your child regulate their sensory output with music, dance, touch, play and movement, food, rest, and quiet spaces are all wonderful proactive tools to help maintain balance and internal regulation for the traumatized child. Regulation is also what is the main goal of empowering strategies discussed in Chapter 4; therefore, the ultimate way to help your child maintain regulation is to use the empowering strategies. Also, don't try to reason with your child, lecture your child, or discuss their behaviors if your child is not "regulated" as your child will certainly not be able to be rational or reason with you. Therefore, our primary goal as a TIFP is always to keep perceived safety in mind to aim for regulation.

Relate

The second R outlined by Dr. Perry is Relate. Once a child is regulated, we want to try to help our child feel connected to us in all interactions, especially at the point of dysregulation. Therefore, TIFPs work toward connection by seeking to relate to their child with sensitive and empathetic parenting practices. These principles were also discussed in Chapter 5 under the "Connecting principles". This is the process of attunement where we connect and relate to our child on an emotional level. Attuned TIFPs are great listeners to their children. They seek to always show empathy, especially at the point of dysregulation. They become aware of their own body language, their voice volume, and their tone, especially when having difficult discussions with their child. It is being in sync with the needs, feelings of your child and being aware of our own interfering behaviors that may disrupt the needs and feelings of our children. Dr. Perry outlines that the "Relate" need is where the limbic system is at work. One way to relate is to acknowledge the feelings of your child. It is also good for you to reassure your child that you support them and are present with them. Using reflective statements such as, "This must be hard for you. I am here for you".

This "relate" need can be difficult for some children with a history of rejection and abandonment. Although they need connection and relationship, your child may push them away from you (at least at first). I can't tell you the number of times my children pushed me away and told me that they did not want me in their life, especially in the early days of placement. Although they pushed me away at first, they desperately wanted and needed to be loved. This push and pull in the relationship was the only way to begin to learn to trust. So, please don't lose hope when your kids may not want to connect with you. Over the long run, it is hoped that they will eventually accept your efforts to connect with you.

Reason

The last R is "Reason". The best time for a TIFP to reason with a child is only when a child is regulated and connected. The problem is as foster parents we sometimes go straight to the reason at the point of dysregulation, and this will backfire for you. By reason, Dr. Perry outlines that we help our child to reflect and learn from their experiences. This is the stage that your child learns to solve problems. However, remember, this can only occur as your child is regulated and connected with you first. This is the stage that the "correcting" strategies discussed in Chapter 7. This is also the place when we need to focus on "re-do's" with your child to help them learn new ways to respond.

According to Perry & Winphrey (2021), this is the work of the cortex part of your brain. The frontal cortex of our brain also helps us to be able to be social and relate to others. In addition, this part of the brain impacts our ability to make choices and understand consequences. It also puts a damper on impulsivity. Disinhibition is the ability to stop an impulse, and this is the work of the frontal cortex. The frontal cortex also helps us to plan, make goals, and organize. Remember, if you want your child to do these things, they must be regulated and connected to you. If regulation or connection is off mark, so will their reasoning and judgment. So, we move from the brain stem to the limbic system, to the cortex. Or said another way, we move from regulation, to relating to reasoning. We cannot expect our children in foster care to reason if they are not regulated and connected to you.

We know that trauma can affect a child's ability to understand cause-and-effect relationships. Think about how a young child learns through healthy attachment. I have a need, it is met! I am struggling and there is someone to comfort me. We cannot expect a child to learn how to self-regulate themselves until first they experience getting their needs met consistently from a caregiver. A child then needs to learn to coregulate with an adult before being expected to self-regulate. However, trauma experiences cause the limbic system to be on alert all the time. This causes the frontal lobe, which is responsible for cause and effect, to be temporarily short-circuited. However, when this happens repeatedly, their front lobes do not develop as quickly. Therefore, we may not be able to expect our child to understand basic cause-and-effect thinking if they have been survivors of ongoing toxic stress! If you want your child to understand how their actions impact others, they must experience healthy forms of coregulation of their needs and attachment with infrequent limbic system activation.

Now, take a moment to reflect on how you would respond when your child uses profanity. Do you provide a calm, reassuring presence? Do you identify with their hurt and provide reassurance to help your child get to the "reason" stage? If you struggle with this, you are not alone. I struggle with this as well. Obviously, you need to address the behavior, but it is better to address the behavior when your child is operating in the frontal lobe of their brain (the thinking part of the brain). There is hope for you to change your behavior knowing how the brain of your traumatized child works. For many parents, this is helpful to avoid the problem of blaming and or labeling your child as a monster or manipulative.

It is important for TIFPs to understand that the result of broken attachment is dysregulation. If a young child has a significant attachment that has been broken (i.e., being removed from birth/first parent, abuse, etc.), it results in dysregulation. A child learns how to self-regulate only when he/she has a significant, healthy attachment person. Therefore, we can expect a child who has a history of neglect, physical, emotional, or sexual abuse to struggle with the ability to regulate themselves quickly or efficiently.

Furthermore, a child learns how to self-regulate themselves after a healthy attachment person in their lives can help them co-regulate. If you or another significant caretaker in the child's life showed signs of dysregulation (signs of disapproval, yelling, lecturing, or dismissiveness) at the point of your child's dysregulation, your child will likely struggle to be able to self-regulate. All in all, the way we respond to a child in a meltdown is to start with empathy to get a child calm and able to think, and then process with your child and do re-do's and discuss options to focus on the "teachable moments" once your child is calm. The timing of this type of teachable moment or "re-do" does matter!

You may want to get the honest feedback of others who see you respond to your child. Take a risk and ask your spouse or close friend to give you honest feedback concerning their perception of your demeanor when your foster/adoptive child is being disruptive or dysregulated. As a single parent, I had to review videotapes of me interacting with my child to find out that I was not always as empathetic and warm with my kids as I imagined in my own mind. It is common for parents to struggle with this kind of thing. It is not easy, but the best parents identify this and seek to make improvements in their own attitudes and behaviors.

Lessons Learned

1. When your child reacts and engages in behavior you do not approve, you need to slow down and show empathy first.
2. It is important for trauma-informed caretakers to be aware of their own facial expressions and tone when their foster/adoptive child is disruptive, oppositional, aggressive, or dysregulated. Respond rather than react!
3. Empathy and attunement are the ingredients to help your son/daughter move from dysregulation to regulation.
4. When the child under your care is regulated, you can then begin the process of practicing the "re-do" and coming up with alternative behaviors to reinforce, encourage, and support.
5. Our kids can become experts of our own nonverbals. Try to become more aware of your nonverbal expressions and posturing that may be intimidating for your child.

Reference

Perry, B.P., & Winphrey, O. (2021). *What Happened to You? Conversations on Trauma, Resilience, and Healing*. Macmillan.

Resisting the Punishment Trap

11

It is a trap to use punishment as the first way to reduce a behavior you want to stop. It is much better to reinforce a behavior you want to see.

Often, punitive consequences are the only thing we know to do with maladaptive behavior; however, there are many other tools to help reduce maladaptive behavior rather than going straight to punitive consequences and punishment-based strategies. Specifically, it is best to reinforce the behaviors you want to see, rather than exclusively punishing the behaviors you do not wish to see. "Harsh punishments and sermons aren't effective for gaining their compliance. At-risk children respond far better to a constructive approach to discipline, one that guides them to think more consciously about choices and consequences without being shamed" (Purvis *et al.*, 2007, p. 91).

Punishment occurs when a consequence follows a behavior that results in a decrease in the future frequency of the behavior. The consequence can be a presentation or a negative consequence (a reprimand, lecture, shouting), which is also known as positive punishment. It can also include the removal of a stimulus (taking away video games, taking away a favorite toy, etc.), which is also referred to as negative punishment (Mayer *et al.*, 2018).

Using punishment for a child with a history of trauma, neglect, and attachment issues can cause more harm than good. Yet, many parents continue to rely upon using punishment. Punishment can be addictive to the parent as it may show a temporary reduction in their child's behavior. This addictive part of punishment can result in a foster/adoptive parent getting caught up in the punishment trap and relying upon it, rather than relying upon positive reinforcement to teach new behaviors.

DOI: 10.4324/9781003601081-15

There are many problems associated with punishment. First, research has proven that punishment has only temporarily suppressed behavior without lasting change (Millenson, 1967; Donnelian *et al.*, 1988; Sidman, 2000; Mayer *et al.*, 2018; Holz *et al.*, 1963). The trap occurs because maladaptive behavior may stop the behavior, but the effects are only temporary. It does not permanently suppress behavior. For example, I may yell at my child and the child immediately stops what he is doing, but the effects of stopping do not truly eliminate the behavior; it only stops it temporarily. It likely will return as soon as the punishment contingencies end.

Second, punishment does not teach new behavior. In other words, we may punish a child, but that only teaches one what to avoid (Donnelian *et al.*, 1988). For example, we could punish a child every time he may use profanity when frustrated, but this does not teach the child how to respond when frustrated. Positive reinforcement is more effective. Positive reinforcement occurs when we provide a consequence following a behavior, which leads to an increase in the future probability of the behavior. There are numerous studies which demonstrate punishment is only effective if combined with positive reinforcement (Mayer *et al.*, 2018). We need to focus on building replacement behaviors. The Ethical Code for Behavior Analysts states, "The behavior analyst recommends reinforcement rather than punishment whenever possible. If punishment procedures are necessary, the behavior analyst always includes reinforcement procedures for alternative behavior in the program" (2016, guideline 4.08). For example, the replacement behavior for profanity may be to use a substitute word such as "rats!". One can use role play and find natural opportunities to prompt and reinforce him/her when he says "Rats" as compared to just punishing your child when he/she may use profanity.

Third, punishment may harm the relationship that you have and want to develop with your foster/adoptive child. The result is that the one being punished may likely try to avoid the one delivering the punishment (Donnelian *et al.*, 1988; Sidman, 2000). It also will likely create a type of conditioned response where negative feelings may develop toward the one that punishes him.

The fourth problem with punishment is the retribution effect. The research shows that the one being punished may become aggressive or engage in retribution/revenge behaviors (as a self-protective measure) when punished (Mayhew & Harris, 1978; Donnelian *et al.*, 1988; Sidman, 2000). In addition to the possibility of increased aggression, it has been shown to increase the risk of antisocial behavior, decreased quality of parent–child relationship, decreased child mental health, and a risk that individual will be abusive to their own child or spouse (Gershoff *et al.*, 2022; Mayer *et al.*, 2018).

With the first few months of taking placement of my children, I recall a situation in which my child got upset at me after I provided him/her with a punitive consequence and went out and got a rock and carved some cuss words on the paint of my car. One child of mine would use a term called, "payback". Payback was when my child was upset with me or someone. For example, when I removed a video game or preferred item, my child would engage in "payback" to me. Fortunately, as attachment was built between my children and I, the "payback" behaviors gradually diminished. All in all, I strongly recommend that you be very careful with using a lot of punishment procedures with your foster/adoptive child, especially as you are attempting to build attachment with your child.

If punishment does not truly eliminate behavior, is there a way to eliminate behavior? Absolutely! There are specific behavioral strategies that foster/adoptive parents can use to reinforce other behaviors they want to see. Behavior analysts call this type of behavior a "replacement behavior". A behavior that serves the same function and gets the same result for the foster/adoptive child. If the behavior we want to eliminate is throwing a temper tantrum to avoid doing their homework, we may have the replacement behavior of "Can I have a break, please?". The replacement behavior of "Can I have a break, please?" has the same function of "escape". So, it is important to reinforce a behavior that has the same function of the maladaptive behavior. If the behavior we want to eliminate is talking too loud in the library, we can reinforce your foster/adoptive child when he/she speaks softly in the library.

If you decide to use punishment, it is important to make it mild and brief. Often, I see signs of a defeated foster/adoptive parent when they just start to increase the level of punishment when it does not permanently eliminate behavior. They take away their child's cell phone or iPad for one day. The behavior returns, so they take it away for three days, now one week, now one month. It is not any more effective to do long-term consequences as compared to doing short-term consequences. Therefore, if you do use punishment, do it in milder and more short term.

Please, please, avoid physical forms of punishment or corporal punishment. This can lead to antisocial behavior, unhealthy forms of fear, physical issues, and physical health problems (Donnelian *et al.*, 1988; Gershoff, 2010; Burt *et al.*, 2021; Heilmann *et al.*, 2021). Gershoff (2010) noted that a meta-analysis indicates that 87% of the research studies on long-term outcomes show that the long-term effects of corporal punishment show that children are less compliant and engage in less moral and positive social behaviors. The risks of using corporal punishment outweigh any temporary benefits.

When thinking about "consequences", it is much better to focus your parenting approach more on the good consequences to increase the behaviors you wish for them to continue (positive reinforcement) than the bad ones for behaviors you do not want to see any more (punishment).

If a child is running around the pool, we can say, "Stop running". However, it is better to say, "Show me how you can use your walking feet". "Wow, great job of using your walking feet!". You are reinforcing the behavior you want to see rather than punishing the behavior you do not want to continue.

Although punishment does not truly teach new behavior, there will be times in which you need to punish a behavior. If Re-do's and reinforcing the positive behavior are not working, you may need to put a consequence such as removing a privilege. If you do this, make sure you continue to reinforce the alternative, replacement behavior in the process. The three laws of logical consequence, as was outlined by Nelson (1985), Related to the Behavior, Respectful, and Reasonable.

1. Related to the Behavior: If a child makes a mess, make him clean it up. This is a natural consequence of the behavior. This is still considered punishment, but it is perfectly appropriate and even advisable in this situation to punish the behavior of making a mess by having him/her clean their mess up.
2. Respectful: As a trauma-informed foster parent, always be kind. Do your best to stay calm, avoid shaming your child, or any displaying attitude or verbal behavior that communicates a message of "I told you so" or "Why didn't you listen to me?'"

3. Reasonable: Long-term consequences are not any more effective than short-term ones. For example, taking away video games or their cell phone for one month is not reasonable. It likely will not do anything to teach new behavior and will not be any more effective than a short-term consequence. It will just create more frustration for your child and result in a barrier in your relationship with your child.

Nelson (2006) expanded the three laws of natural consequences to four laws by adding another "R", which was "Revealed in Advance". If you use consequences, it is best to set up the consequences ahead of time. For example, you can say, I will purchase you a phone if you obey these simple guidelines. I will allow you to use the cell phone if you do not view porn. If you view porn, you will lose your cell phone for three days. In this situation, you and your child have made a reasonable agreement ahead of time of the consequence that will be imposed upon your child for a specific behavior.

Otherwise, if you rely upon your punishment, Nelson (2006) identifies the following 4 "Rs" of punishment:

1. Resentment ("I will hold this against you and not forget it")
2. Revenge ("I will get them back for this!")
3. Rebellion ("I will win by doing things my own way")
4. Retreat ("I will distance myself from you")

Punishment can be effective if done in the right way. You should not use punishment as your go-to strategy; it needs to be used sparingly (only if other reinforcement-based strategies alone do not reduce the maladaptive behavior). Punishment should only be used if you reinforce alternative behaviors (Holz et al., 1963). "If punishment is employed as an attempt to eliminate certain behavior, then whatever reinforcement the undesirable behavior has led to must be made available via a more desirable behavior. Merely punishing school children for misbehavior in class may have little permanent effect" (Millenson, 1967, p. 429).

For example, if you punish a child for running around the pool by sitting out of the pool for a period of five minutes, this is considered a punishment procedure. However, this procedure will likely not be as effective unless you make special attempts to reinforce the alternative behavior of walking around the pool. Another example, if you reprimand a child for taking food without permission, you can find opportunities to reinforce the behavior copiously when they ask permission for food.

All in all, punishment cannot be avoided altogether, but it certainly needs to be limited. For kids with trauma histories, it is best to avoid punishment contingencies including consequences of lectures, reprimands, taking away privileges, and yelling. Avoid corporal forms of punishment (especially for children with trauma histories) as this provides more harm than good (Heilmann *et al.*, 2021). Whenever possible, reinforcement contingencies are the way to go!

If you have teens, sometimes it can be hard to reach them. Parents will see much better success if they go out of their way to have positive, pleasant experiences with their teens (and younger children as well). Really make intentional effort to have dozens of these types of positive interactions every day. A negative environment in your home will kill the mood and your relationship with your teen. Unfortunately, I have talked to hundreds of parents, especially older youth, and I have found that there is a trend where parents acknowledge that there are more negative interactions than positive ones. Parents are reporting increasing levels of frustration with their teens. When they do interact with their teens, it tends to be by showing signs of disapproval. It is important to know that when we attend to maladaptive behavior (such as disrespect, eye rolls, and sighs), we can also run the risk of strengthening the behavior by our reaction. In other words, it is possible to inadvertently reinforce your child's maladaptive behavior based upon our reaction. In this case, it may be much better to ignore the behavior in the moment. Once the situation is long and gone, we can provide an opportunity for a "re-do". However, research shows that it is much better to give attention to the positive behaviors your children do than to give attention to the maladaptive behaviors. All in all, sometimes, it is best to just ignore certain behaviors!

Lessons Learned

1. Never lose sight of the fact that there will likely be potential, negative side effects of using punishment with your foster/adoptive child, especially when attachment is not yet fully developed.
2. Research shows that reinforcing the behaviors you want to see is much more effective as compared to just punishing the behaviors you do not want to see. Let the research guide your behaviors as a parent by focusing more on the positive!

3. If you do resort to using punishment, make sure you lavish lots of reinforcement on the behavior that you want to see. Don't forget the 4 to 1 praise-to-correction ratio.
4. Pick your battles! In some situations, it is better to just ignore the behavior and create a more positive environment than run the risk of another negative interaction with your child.
5. If you do provide a negative consequence for your child, try to use a natural consequence when possible.
6. If you do provide a negative consequence for your child, allow your adopted child to have a choice. For example, you can say, "Would you rather lose your cell phone for 2 hours or write 15 sentences that say, 'I will ask permission to leave the home'"?

References

Behavior Analyst Certification Board. (2020). *Ethics Code for Behavior Analysts*. https://bacb.com/wp-content/ethics-code-for-behavior-analysts

Burt, A., Clark, D. A., & Hyde, L.W. (2021). Twin Differences in Harsh Parenting Predict Youth's Antisocial Behavior. *Psychol Sci.* 32 (3), 395–409.

Donnelian, A.M., Lavigne, G.W., Negri, S., & Fassbender, L.L. (1988). *Progress without Punishment: Effective Approaches for Learners with Behavior Problems*. Teachers College Press.

Gershoff, E.T. (2010). More Harm than Good: A Summary of Scientific Research on the Intended and Unintended Effects of Corporal Punishment on Children. *Law Contempt Probl.* 73 (2), 31–56.

Gershoff, E.T., Cuartas, J., Bailey, D.H., & McCoy, D.C. (2022). Physical Punishment and Child, Adolescent, and Adult Outcomes in Low- and Middle-Income Countries: Protocol for Systematic Review and Meta-Analysis. *Syst Rev,* 11.

Heilmann, A., Mehay, A., Watt, R.G., Kelly, Y., Durrant, J.E., Turnhout, J.V., & Gershoff, E.T. (2021). Physical Punishment and Child Outcomes: a Narrative Review of Prospective Studies. *Lancelot,* 398, 355–364.

Holz, W.Z., Azrin, N.H., & Ayllon, T. (1963). Elimination of Behavior of Mental Patients by Response Produced Extinction. *J Exp Anal Beh.* 6(3), 407–412.

Mayer, R.C., Azaroff-Sulzer, B., & Wallace, C. (2018). *Behavior Analysis for Lasting Change*, 4th edition, Sloan publishing.

Mayhew, G.L., & Harris, F.C. (1978). Some Negative Side Effects of a Punishment Procedure for Stereotyped Behavior. *J Behav Ther Exp Psychiatry.* 9(3), 245–251. https://doi.org/10.1016/0005-7916(78)90036-8.

Millenson, J.R. (1967). *Principles of Behavior Analysis*. Macmillan.

Nelson, J. (2006). *Positive Discipline*. Ballantine Books.

Nelson, J. (1985). The Three Rs of Logical Consequences, the Three R's of Punishment, and the Six Steps for Winning Children Over. *Individual Psychology: Journal of Adlerian Theory, Research & Practice.* 41 (2), 161–165.

Purvis, K.B., Cross, D.R., & Sunshine, W.L. (2007). *The Connected Child*. McGraw Hill.

Sidman, M. (2000). *Coercion and Its Fallout*. Authors Cooperative.

Repairing the Rupture **12**

Nothing hurts more than the effects of a collapse in a relationship. Hurtful words, conflict and anger, and distancing behaviors are inevitable and can have lasting impact upon child and parent. A rupture in a relationship will have effects on the physical and emotional development of you and your child. We know that the stress of a shattered connection can weaken the immune system, alter cardiovascular function, and impact hormone levels. In addition, conflict and broken relationships can drastically alter the limbic system of the brain, which is the command system of emotion (Lewis *et al.*, 2001). We know that rupture can result in the dysregulation of the body and emotions; however, the wonderful news is that wherever there is a rupture, there is an opportunity for a repair. The repair will help to recalibrate the limbic systems of all involved and restore order and harmony.

Some of us grew up in an environment where there were a lot of ruptures but limited repairs between parent and child. However, it's critical for foster parents to repair the hurts in their relationships with the children in their care. When a rupture occurs, sometimes we turn away from each other instead of turning toward each other, but this only leads to resentment. On the other hand, a rupture-repair relationship seeks to address ruptures and make amends. A rupture-resentment relationship occurs if we don't seek to repair what is damaged.

---

*Some extraordinarily beautiful things can come
after a rupture that would never have occurred*

DOI: 10.4324/9781003601081-16

without the rupture. But it takes a lot of work and humility on your part. Intimacy is built when a rupture is followed by repair. We may not be able to prevent the rupture, but we can surely repair it.

Redemption can come from a broken relationship. It is out of the brokenness that we get to see new hope, fresh intimacy, and redemption. Beauty can come from brokenness!

If repair doesn't happen, it leads to distance and a lack of connection in your relationship with your foster/adoptive child. It also subtly communicates a message to your child under your care that you don't care about the relationship enough to try to mend it. Working toward repair can be difficult and vulnerable, but it is so worth it! M. Scott Peck says that intimacy only comes through the tunnel of chaos and conflict (Peck, 1978). Relationships cannot happen without conflict. Conflict isn't fun, but the most important part of the conflict is the ability to make amends and repair. When done correctly, it can be very rewarding.

Ruptures between children and parents are inevitable, especially between foster/adoptive children and their foster/adoptive parents. However, when they happen, we have a choice. One option is to avoid it and not talk about it. We may think this is a safer approach. However, intimacy cannot occur in this situation. A second option is to focus on your child's behavior without taking responsibility for your own behavior. Unfortunately, this is what I tend to do when I'm frustrated with my children's behavior. However, you do not want to model such behavior. The third and best option is to apologize and to engage in behaviors and words that help repair the damage. We may not be able to prevent the rupture, but we can certainly repair it.

Sometimes, as a foster parent, I have failed miserably. When my son or daughter is disrespectful to me or calls me inappropriate names in a moment of frustration, I respond by raising my voice or saying things that make things worse rather than better. At such moments, my mistake is directing my attention to how my child should have responded rather than taking ownership for my own behavior. I have blown things so many times. However, parents need redo's too! The most important part of messing things up is putting them back together.

As hard as it is, apologizing and asking your child to forgive you is the best thing to do.

After all, you are modeling the behavior you want your child to display to you and others.

If you had a role in the hurt, a repair includes several ingredients.

1. Listen and show empathy to your foster/adoptive child. This includes acknowledging their hurt and/or attempting to gather more information about it.
2. Identify your role in the hurt.
3. Apologize.
4. Forgive your child and move forward in your relationship.

After the rupture, you may need to give your child some space. When you think you and your child might be ready to address the issue, say something like, "Is now a good time to talk?" If they say, "Go away!", respond with something like, "Okay, I'll give you some space, but I'd like to talk to you later, okay?"

It's critical to listen and empathize with your child's experience, even if you don't agree with their interpretation of the situation. Don't dismiss their feelings. This can be difficult when you're frustrated in the moment. However, it's important for you to empathize first with their concerns and experiences before addressing your concerns about their response. One of my favorite sayings comes from author Stephen Covey: "Seek first to understand, then to be understood". I'm not always the best at this, especially when my children are being disrespectful to me, so it takes a lot of work for all of us to be consistent at this.

Identifying your role in the rupture is important, but you also need to address your child's role. A rupture always involves at least two parties. When your child does mess up, it is critical for your child to know that no blunder is big enough for you to stop loving them!

However, if your child does make a big blunder, you need to listen and understand and take responsibility for any behaviors that you may have contributed to in their blunder. When you do this, your child will be more likely to listen and take responsibility for their behaviors.

Trauma-informed, empathetic parenting requires a lot of discipline. You will make mistakes along the way. The best thing to do when a rupture occurs is to apologize and to ask for forgiveness. I'm not always the best at this. Sometimes my focus is on my child's behavior and what I want them to do differently. In the process, I fail to model what I would like my child to do.

When I'm so focused on trying to "change" my son or daughter's behavior, I'm missing the mark. Instead, my key focus needs to be on connection and making amends first.

By doing this, I am modeling what I want my own child to do, which is to take ownership of his or her behavior.

Apologies are a necessary ingredient for your child to feel safe, establish a connection with you, and rebound from ruptures.

When making an apology, be specific. Don't just say, "I'm sorry". Instead, say, "I know I raised my voice at you when I was frustrated. That's not the response I wanted. I realize that hurt you. I hope you can forgive me, and I'll try to work on that in the future". Apologizing is about naming your behavior, owning it, and highlighting how you think it impacted the other person. This is what empathetic foster parenting is all about – apologizing, forgiving, and letting go so that true connection and intimacy can occur. In addition, when you apologize, forgive, and let go, you model the behavior you want to see from your children.

Moving forward means that you will try not to bring it up again. If you constantly bring up past behaviors, your child will tune you out. Moving forward means you will not live in shame, and you won't force your child to do so either. The goal is to rebuild your relationship with your child and create a greater sense of connection and intimacy.

As foster parents, it's easy to get caught in the trap of focusing only on the behavior you want your child to change, especially when your child is shifting blame or avoiding responsibility. In the process, you may lose your cool. Instead, take the first step by apologizing for your behavior and then asking your child if there's anything they could have done differently. When you take responsibility for your behavior, your child will be more likely to learn how to take responsibility for their own.

In between meltdowns, challenges, hurts, and ruptures, it's important to memorialize the successes that you and your child share.

Some parents keep a box or a journal with notes about the little successes they enjoy with their child. I have kept a journal for my kids, noting the positive things I see them doing over the years. Unfortunately, I'm not always as disciplined at this as I would like to be. When you feel everything is falling apart, it's great to go back and read the notes of encouragement and review your child's successes. Memorializing each success helps to paint your child not as an evil little gremlin who constantly gets in trouble but as a child who is slowly developing, growing, and learning new skills. Don't forget that two steps forward and one step back is still progress!

Lifebooks can also be a great way for children in foster care to process their history and experiences. A lifebook is a personalized type of journal for children in foster care to reflect upon their experiences and their family history. This can be a great opportunity (when appropriate) for children to document their family tree for their birth/first parents and their new family tree with their adopted family. The lifebooks can also contain pictures, photos, drawings, and special memories for the child. This can be a great way for your child to seek to find some repair from their own hurts and process their feelings and emotions. Many children in foster care can develop disconnected memories about their past, so it is a good way to help a child find their purpose and identity in relationship to their past and future.

Do you know how to eat an elephant? One bite at a time. The problem is, sometimes, we get overwhelmed by all the ruptures and how big that elephant is. That's why it's important to step back and assess your progress, no matter how small. Hey, I just ate the toenail!

When repairing a rupture, make self-care a priority as well. Compassion fatigue occurs when we spend all our time caring for others in the absence of self-care. Many foster/adoptive parents who are reading this book right now are likely experiencing the signs and symptoms of compassion fatigue. Figley (2002) outlines some of the symptoms of compassion fatigue:

- Feeling tired all the time
- Disrupted sleep
- Gastrointestinal issues
- Feeling disconnected from others
- Reduced motivation
- Lack of purpose
- Mental exhaustion

We can all learn from the example of Mother Theresa. She understood compassion fatigue. It was mandatory for her nuns to take one year off every four to five years to allow them time to recover from the effects of their care to others.

Lessons Learned

1. Respect your child's need for space before demanding an apology.
2. Make apologies when appropriate. You can't expect your child to apologize to you if you never apologize to your child. For example, you can say, "I really messed up here as when I yelled at you. I am sorry the way that impacted you. I need to do better. Do you forgive me?"
3. After a rupture, find special opportunities to reconnect with your child.
4. If you start to become discouraged with the behaviors of your child, reflect on the positives. It may be a good idea to create a jar full of positive notes and reminders about the beauty of your child that you can review after a rupture.

References

Lewis, T., Amini, F., & Lannon, R. (2001). *A General Theory of Love*. Vintage Publishing.

Figley, C.R. (2002). Compassion Fatigue: Psychotherapists Chronic Lack of Self-Care. *J ClinPsychol*. 58(11), 1433–1441.

Peck, S.M. (1978). *The Road Less Traveled: A New Psychology of Love, Traditional Values and Spiritual Growth*. Simon & Schuster.

Perry, B.P., & Winphrey, O. (2021). *What Happened to You? Conversations on Trauma, Resilience, and Healing*. Macmillan.

Section IV

Behavioral Challenges in Trauma-Informed Foster Parenting

This is not necessarily meant to be a precise field manual for behavioral challenges, but it will provide you with practical suggestions and feedback for common maladaptive behaviors that are observed among foster/adoptive children. In this section, we will look at teaching strategies to teach new behavior, proactive strategies to prevent behavior, and response strategies when the behavior occurs. It should be noted that often times we tend to rely upon responding strategies to try to change behavior, but it is important to not lose sight of proactive and teaching strategies in the process. It is important to respond based upon the function of each behavior, so we will look at how our response may alter depending upon the function of the behavior.

DOI: 10.4324/9781003601081-17

Homework Battles 13

> Choose attachment over educational success. It is important to not have such a high expectation for academic performance if it comes at the price of broken attachment.

World War III erupted in our household between my son and I over homework in the early days of his placement. I never imagined how difficult and stressful things would turn out over this issue. I imagined a situation in which my children would come home and do his homework with mild or moderate frustration and then have fun doing the things he enjoyed afterward. After all, that was my experience growing up. I was always eager to get my homework as soon as I got home, so I could enjoy the rest of my day. Once again, my idealistic expectations came crashing down.

Neither Andrew nor Kayla had experience doing homework. In their previous foster home, they were not expected to do homework after school. Both of my children had some significant academic delays, but his will largely in part to their lack of exposure to academics. They had never been exposed to a household that had high expectations for academic excellence, so coming to my home was a big cultural adjustment for them. Unfortunately, I was unprepared for how hard it would be to get my kids invested in their education. Therefore, I didn't do the best job of facilitating this cultural adjustment for my kids.

To provide some outside support, I enrolled my children in an academic program called Kumon to help them learn to read. In my idealistic view, I thought it would inspire them to pursue excellence in education. Sounds lovely, right? The problem was, this was my value, not theirs.

DOI: 10.4324/9781003601081-18

------

*My values were as foreign to them as living in a
country with a different language.*

My desire for them to excel academically came at a cost, but I learned quickly and changed my approach. A key realization occurred when I saw how a simple instruction to do their homework or when I turned off the television for homework time would erupt into a battle. One of my children ended up breaking the television. And a few months later, another one was broken! I also began to realize that there were much better things to emphasize as compared to good grades. Practicing kindness and showing generosity were traits that I decided to focus on more compared to making sure that all their homework was complete. I wanted to focus more on connection than good grades.

------

*I changed my approach to focus more on giggles,
playing, swimming, and positive interactions. As
my approach changed, the behaviors of my child
also changed!*

I was able to create a positive environment for my child to learn new skills. My child was a great kid who simply had not learned skills to express their disappointments or handle stressful situations.

One of my children had experienced significant struggles behaviorally at school. My child's, the teacher was an "old school" type who believed in using negative consequences to enforce behavior. When my child was disruptive in class, would make my child write out the Declaration of Independence at home. At first, I obliged, but that approach resulted in a broken television, meltdowns, and aggressive behavior. In addition, I was feeling defeated and unproductive as a parent in having all the homework battles; thus, it was a "lose-lose" approach to parenting.

After some reflection, I realized my expectation for my child to follow through with the consequence of writing the Declaration of Independence was breaking my attachment with my child and causing an abundance of heartache. In the process, my child started to project their frustrations onto me. I discussed the situation with my child's teacher and shared that I was.... no longer going to expect my child to do this. My child's teacher didn't understand, and I concluded that the teacher thought I was a terrible parent for not holding my child accountable for their behaviors at home. That was hard for me to take, as I valued my reputation. However, over time, I was able to surrender my pride and let it be. I realized, I couldn't control what teachers, other parents, professionals, bystanders, or even friends thought of the way I parented. I also asked myself what was more important: building attachment and bonding with my children or having them to complete their homework?

I learned to move slowly in my academic expectations, and I believe that was the best decision for all of us. Instead of having my child complete an entire math worksheet, my new goal was for my child to complete just three problems. Gradually, as trust grew, I was able to help raise the bar for my child.

I had already experienced broken televisions, meltdowns, and verbal and physical attacks by asking my child to complete their homework, so something had to change. When I told my child's teacher that I was not going to expect my child to complete all their homework but that I would gradually increase my expectations, the teacher said something like that my child was "a smart kid and they can do it". The teacher didn't understand that I was in the business of building attachments first. I needed to build a sense of trust and safety with my child before setting educational goals. Also, my child probably liked me advocating for their needs. My child saw me advocating for them, which showed them that I had their best interest in mind. Looking back now, I think this was one of the wisest things I did in my early days of fostering. I lowered my expectations regarding homework and then gradually increased them while building my attachment with my children.

The procedure I used with my child was called differential negative reinforcement alternative (DNRA) (Goehring, 2018). Basically, this means I allowed my child to escape the rest of their homework after completing an alternative response, which was completing three problems instead of the entire math worksheet. As my child progressed, I increased the requirement to five problems and eventually the entire worksheet. After that I set an expectation for my child to do their math homework along with ten minutes of reading and then writing a two- to three-sentence summary of what he read. Eventually, my child did their math, reading, and spelling. It took approximately seven to ten months until they were able to do all their homework. In addition to helping my child meet their educational requirements, this DNRA procedure helped me build an attachment with my child, which was my goal. At the same time, it allowed my child to adjust to the new expectation of homework at their own pace. A win-win! In the process, not only did my expectations have to change, so did the value I placed on my ego and how my child's teacher perceived me as a parent.

Remember, there are three ways to change behaviors – teaching strategies, proactive strategies, and response strategies. Teaching strategies are what you do as a trauma-informed parent to teach new skills for your child. Proactive strategies are things you do before the behavior occurs to avoid the behavior. Response strategies are how you respond after the behavior occurs.

As discussed before, the main functions or purposes that behavior serves include escape, attention, sensory, and access (to tangible or intangible items) (Cooper *et al.*, 2020). A behavior's function can be better understood by examining the context in which it takes place. Once you understand the function or purpose of a behavior, you can develop a plan to help your child.

Let's assume the behaviors we see with homework battles, such as not completing their homework, protesting the need to do the homework, or lying about what needs to be done are avoidant behaviors. Your child is trying to escape/avoid doing the homework. We can't truly know that the function of the behavior is escape without analyzing the contingencies in the environment, but for this purpose, I will assume the goal of such behaviors is escape.

Teaching Strategies

For escape-maintained behaviors (i.e- behaviors that are used to escape homework), we will want to teach our child in foster care how to engage in other behaviors to gain escape. This may include helping children learn new skills like asking for help, asking for a break, or asking for more time before starting their homework. The goal is to create an environment where you reinforce your child when they do these types of behaviors. You may need to remind your children that if they get frustrated if they would like to request a break or help, they can always ask.

Teaching self-management strategies can be a great teaching tool for some older children and teens. Many parents of teens who come to my office express frustration that they are constantly having to nag their teens to do their homework. In this type of situation, I talk with the teen as a psychologist, and I ask them if they feel their foster parents nag at them. Interestingly, I never hear a "no" response to that question. I follow up and ask them if they would like it so their foster/adoptive parent would not nag at them. Once again, I never receive a "no" response to that question. I then proceed to outline a "no nag zone". For example, there is a "no nag" zone for homework between 3 pm to 5 pm. However, at 5 pm, if the teen has not started their homework, their parents have permission to "nag" them. I then proceed to tell the teen to set an alarm on their cell phone and allow the cell phone to nag them at 4:50 pm to remind them to do their homework. In this case, a child's behavior of doing their homework is done to avoid the nag from their parents. This can be a great way to teach self-management skills for your child.

Proactive Strategies

For escape-maintained behaviors, proactive strategies are geared toward helping create an environment where the child under your care will be less likely to escape their homework. These strategies are things you do as a trauma-informed foster parent (TIFP) that are designed to help prevent the maladaptive behavior from occurring in the first place. It is a way for you to be a step ahead as you expect the possibility of a challenge and engage in a strategy to help prevent a particular maladaptive behavior from occurring.

For escape-maintained behaviors, our proactive strategies will be geared at helping create an environment where your child will be less likely to escape their homework. In addition to DNRA, chunking can be a great strategy for children who get overwhelmed by homework. Chunking is a proactive behavioral tool we can use to break down a complex activity into smaller parts. For example, if your foster/adoptive child has 20 math problems to do, you may want to ask your child to complete only 10 math problems and then take a break. He/she can then complete the rest after the break. I used chunking frequently when was younger by only showing the small portion of homework that had to complete in one sitting (rather than the entire math worksheet. For example, if there was a math worksheet with 6 problems on it, I would fold the paper in half and only show my child 3 problems. I would say, "Let's just do these 3 problems only". After a break, my child would come back and complete the rest. The chunking strategy may help the homework become a little less anxiety-provoking for our kiddos.

The premack principle is a wonderful proactive strategy to avoid the homework battle. It becomes very difficult to get a child to stop video games to do homework, so the premack contingency can help. The main idea of the premack contingency is to set up the environment of a "First, then" contingency. In the premack contingency, the "then" behavior is considered the preferred activity that reinforces the "first" behavior. For example, we can set up a contingency and say, "First you do 30 minutes of homework, then you can play video games". The "then behavior" is contingent only if the "first" behavior is done. In this example, your child will not be able to watch the television or do their screen time until they first complete their homework. When parents learn how to set up privileges as a contingency, it can drastically help motivate your child to do less preferred tasks.

Providing choices for your child is another proactive strategy to avoid the meltdowns and frustrations related to homework. In choice-making, we can help our children in foster care find some control when they feel they have lost all forms of control. For example, TIFPs can provide a choice as to whether they work like to do their math homework or do their reading first. If you hope your child will read for 30 minutes, you can offer that as a choice by asking "Would you rather read 30 minutes of 45 minutes?" Be creative in empowering your child with choices.

Helping your child develop a consistent routine within a conducive environment can be an effective proactive strategy as well. Consistency helps your child to know what to expect which can help reduce anxiety and resistance. Perhaps, you can have a consistent schedule where your child gets a 15 to 25-minute break when coming home to eat a snack, then he/she does his homework for 1 hour. After homework, your child can have some free time to play video games for 30 minutes to an hour. It is also important to minimize the distractions during homework. Yes, that means away from the cell phone for a brief time! Furthermore, it is important to have a quiet, well-lit space for your foster/adoptive child to do their homework.

As foster/adoptive parents, it is better to focus on the effort of your child as compared to only focusing on the results. Providing an encouraging and supportive environment so you can celebrate the small successes and create a positive environment. Your support can help your child to persevere through challenging assignments and help to reduce defiance as well.

Another great proactive strategy to avoid the homework battle is priming (especially for younger children). Through priming, you state your expectations of what you expect to see to help prepare your child for what is to come. For example, you can say to your child in foster care, "I want to remind you that you will need to start your math homework in 15 minutes. Would you like a snack first". Notice in this situation, you used the strategy of priming and choice-making.

Let's look at the following situations to see how proactive strategies can be used to help prevent major homework battles from erupting.

Situation One:

FOSTER PARENT	It's time to do your homework. Please get started.
CHILD	No! I hate it! Go away!
FOSTER PARENT	That's not the way to talk to me. You must use respect. If you don't do your homework, you'll lose your video game privileges for the rest of the day!
CHILD	You're so mean!

In this situation, everything went awry. This escalation could have been avoided by using proactive strategies of priming, choice-making, and the premack contingency.

Situation Two:

FOSTER PARENT	When we come home today, I know you probably will want to have some wind-down time before doing your homework. How much time do you need before starting your homework? (choice making and priming)
CHILD	Can I have thirty minutes?
FOSTER PARENT	Absolutely, that sounds like a great plan (giving a "yes" and being supportive). Also, once you finish your homework, you're welcome to play video games. (Premack contingency).

Situation Three:

Here is another good example of a foster parent who is using effective proactive strategies.

After your child comes home from school, you can say the following.

PARENT	Wow, you look like you had a hard day. Would you like an apple? (Note: empowering principle)
CHILD	Sure!

PARENT	Okay. I know you'll want to have some wind-down time. How much time do you need before starting your homework? (Note: decision-making principle).
CHILD	Two hours.
PARENT	I realize homework isn't always fun, but we have soccer practice at four o'clock, and I'm concerned you won't have enough time. How about you take a thirty-minute break and then get started on your math homework? After that you can go to soccer practice.
CHILD	I guess so.
PARENT	Once you finish your math homework, if we have enough time, we can get some ice cream before soccer practice. Does that sound like a good plan? (Premack: homework first, then ice cream; creating ownership by asking, "Does that sound like a plan?)
CHILD	Yes, I'll make sure I finish my math homework before soccer.
PARENT	That's a great plan. Let me know if you need any help. I'm here for you, champ!

Some parents may be concerned that getting ice cream after homework is complete is a form of bribery. However, I disagree, seeing as the child is not engaging in maladaptive behavior at the time. If a child were having a tantrum and refusing to do their homework, and I responded by offering to get them ice cream if they did, that would be bribery. Such responses to maladaptive behavior can be avoided!

Response Strategies

If your child starts to get frustrated with their homework, show empathy and acknowledge your child's frustrations and feelings in the moment. Then, process their initial reaction once they are calm and are operating in their prefrontal lobe/thinking part of the brain. Offering choices can provide your child with a sense of control as well.

Here's an example of these behavioral principles at work.

FOSTER PARENT	In about fifteen minutes, you need to start your homework.
CHILD	Go away! I'm not doing it today!

FOSTER PARENT	I hear your frustration. I didn't like doing homework when I was your age either. Sounds like you need some space. Are you asking or telling me to go away? (Here, I'm showing empathy and trying to prompt the child to ask me nicely for a break/replacement behavior.)
CHILD	I'm asking.
FOSTER PARENT	Can you please ask nicely?
CHILD	Can you please go away so I can have a break?
FOSTER PARENT	Absolutely. I will allow you to have a break for 10 minutes. But you will have to start your homework in 10 minutes. Would you like some juice or a snack in the meantime? (The goal here is empowering and decision-making.)
CHILD	Yes, please.
FOSTER PARENT	Great, I'm on it! (Goal: reinforcing behavior and supporting the child.)

Lesson Learned

1. It's much better to focus on attachment than homework battles.
2. For educationally resistant children, advocate for your child to see if they can be accommodated by doing less homework in the early stages of the placement, so you can build attachment.
3. Set routines. Allow some brief downtime when coming home from school, but then set an expectation of doing homework.
4. Create a special place for your child to do homework. Minimize distractions during homework time (e.g., no TV or other screens). If possible, set up a contingency where the cell phone goes into a basket and can be accessed after homework is complete.
5. Set clear, consistent expectations with some structure. For example, give your child a thirty-minute break when they get home during which they can have a snack and relax before doing homework.
6. Take breaks when doing homework. The pomodoro technique involves setting a timer and taking a five-minute break after twenty-five minutes of work. After four breaks, take a fifteen- to twenty-minute break.

References

Cooper, J.O., Heron, T.E., & Heward, W. L. (2020). *Applied Behavior Analysis*, 3rd edition. Pearson Education.

Goehring, N. (2018). *Efficacy of Differential Negative Reinforcement of Alternative Behaviors to Increase Reading Comprehension. Public Access Theses and Dis*sertations from the College of Education and Human Sciences. University of Nebraska.

Responding to Meltdowns and Defiance

14

It is important to see your child's defiance as an opportunity to teach new skills and meet the needs of your child. Strict discipline likely will backfire! Restricting freedoms and losing privileges only result in a greater deficit to our child's need. When possible, it is best to do the opposite of restriction by finding ways to give more choice and more empowerment. This is a counter intuitive parenting strategy but a must for a child with trauma history.

Have you ever heard your child yell or scream the following?

- I can't do it, I am too overwhelmed! (Leading to a Meltdown)

or

- No, I am not going to do that! You can't make me because you are not my mom!!! (Defiance)

These kinds of outbursts can be common for foster and adoptive children. When many children feel cornered into doing something they may not want to do, they may resort to either a meltdown or defiant behavior.

Meltdowns tend to be more involuntary responses based upon antecedent stimuli. Defiance tends to be more deliberate and learned.

A "meltdown" is a broad term that can be defined as the behaviors that result from an overwhelming reaction to sensory or environmental

DOI: 10.4324/9781003601081-19

stimuli. An example of sensory overload may be when a child becomes overstimulated with too many noises or crowded spaces. In addition, strong emotions such as anger, fear, or sadness may trigger a meltdown. If a child in your foster home feels misunderstood or unsupported, they may develop overload of certain environmental stimuli and have a meltdown. Fatigue and hunger can play a significant role in emotional regulation as well. If an individual is stressed and tired, he/she will likely have a great challenge in coping with stress. Often times, a child may become overstimulated with things, resulting in meltdown behavior such as crying, screaming, hitting self or others, etc.

Defiant behavior is also common for children with trauma histories, but, at times, it can be observed in all children. However, for children with trauma histories, defiance can be with a greater intensity and greater frequency than for children without trauma histories. Defiance can take many forms including showing resistance to authority, refusal to comply with requests and rules, arguing, and meltdowns when presented with non-preferred tasks. It can be quite frustrating for parents to deal with defiance. Children with defiance tend to naturally cause chaos around their house as they have the need to be in control of all things.

Defiant behavior can be problematic for parents; however, the defiant behavior is not necessarily a problem or challenging for the child.

Obviously, a child's defiance will have negative outcomes including the possibility of disrupting their friends and interfering with their learning in the school. It can also be a barrier for greater attachment between parent and child. Although these outcomes are certainly problematic, a child may not necessarily understand or view these things as problematic. Therefore, I use the term "maladaptive behavior" as compared to "problematic behavior" or "challenging behavior".

Often, foster/adoptive parents of oppositional and defiant children view their child as being "manipulative". They may also consider their child with frequent meltdowns as lacking self-control. However, these types of labels you may provide for your son/daughter may only result in you seeking to provide more strict discipline for your child due to your belief about your child. Instead, it is important to understand that a defiant or dysregulated child who has a meltdown is likely no more manipulative than anyone else, but they have learned to get their needs met by their behavior. In fact, often, a child with a trauma history may be using defiance or meltdowns to survive in that moment! It may be the quick work of the amygdala of their brain. When a child is controlling and defiant or emotionally overstimulated, he/she likely is simply trying to gain a sense of safety.

A child who is experiencing a meltdown may have the following thinking patterns:

- Life is too unpredictable.
- Things are too overwhelming for me.
- I do not know what to do.

However, your child is not thinking too much during a meltdown. They can't think as their limbic system short circuits their prefrontal lobe/thinking part of their brain.

A defiant child may be experiencing the following thinking patterns:

- I cannot trust you.
- If I lose control, I may get hurt.
- I will just increase my level of control to feel safe.

Being told "no" or being redirected may be a reminder of your child's loss of control that occurred through their trauma experience. Often, children have learned to equate being in control with safety. When the child is not "in control", they have experienced harm in the past. When a child has lost all sense of control and power, they have learned to try to control their environment to feel safe. When this has been repeated, it can literally change their functioning of their brain and result in all kinds of defiant behaviors and meltdowns as well.

Teaching Strategies

For meltdowns

For every behavior you want to decrease, you need to find the corresponding behavior to reinforce (the replacement behavior) that serves the same purpose/function of the maladaptive behavior. Acknowledging and reinforcing desirable behavior helps to motivate your child to repeat such actions. Therefore, understanding the triggers provides a blueprint for developing strategies to prevent meltdowns.

In many cases, the function of meltdown behaviors serves a function of escape. Your child is likely trying to escape the uncomfortable feeling of intense emotions in that moment. In many situations, after a child has a meltdown, their body and mind may feel more relaxed. If you think about it, meltdowns kind of make sense! You feel overwhelmed, so you engage in meltdown behaviors of crying, screaming, etc., to escape the internal tension in the moment.

It is critical for trauma-informed foster parents (TIFPs) to remain calm and to be aware of your own triggers when your child in foster care is having a meltdown.

Your response can either escalate or deescalate the situation.

For escape-maintained meltdowns, TIFPs seek to try to teach new skills to help your child learn to escape their uncomfortable feelings. Some of these new skills may be things like:

1. Learning to communicate their frustration with their words
2. Learning to release their frustration in more adaptive ways (squeezing a squishy ball, exercising, screaming or hitting into a pillow, etc.).

For defiance

I will assume that the purpose of defiant and noncompliant behavior is "escape". Your child wants to escape a nonpreferred task or instruction. Knowing this, the replacement behavior needs to serve the same function of escape. However, it is important to realize that the function of the noncompliant behavior may not always be escaped. For example, sometimes, children may engage in noncompliance to gain attention or gain a sense of safety in their own lives.

Here are some possible replacement behaviors to reinforce for escape-maintained defiance:

1. Asking for help
2. Asking to delay the task or asking to take a break
3. Negotiating the expectation (i.e., if asked to do read for 20 minutes, your child can be taught to ask to only read for 15 minutes)

Therefore, we want to give a lot of opportunities for your foster/adoptive child to role-play and practice the above skills. This may be providing a hypothetical scenario for your child to identify the best course of action. It may be fun and playful to act out a particular alternative response with your child that you hope for them to do in the future.

Proactive Strategies

For meltdowns

TIFPs are proactive and intervene to support their child as soon as possible. Sometimes, a child can be so overwhelmed that he/she goes from 0 to 90 in two seconds; however, often, as a detective, you may be able to see some signs of when your child is about to have a meltdown and intervene at that point. There are times in which it becomes too late to show any success as you may just have to wait until your child has their release in the meltdown; however, the key is to intervene before you get to that point.

TIFPs become masters at meeting needs. See the need and then meet the need. So, a proactive strategy to avoid meltdowns is to meet the needs before your child unravels.

For defiance

One proactive strategy that I encourage parents of oppositional children to use is called the <u>Basket strategy</u> outlined by Ross Greene (1998). outlined using three baskets from non negotiable, to negotiable, to negligable baskets (not with the battle) I refer to these three baskets as the "yes" Bucket, "no" Bucket, and "compromise" bucket. Anytime you say, "yes", to your foster/adoptive child you place a token, object, marble, or coin in the "Yes" Bucket/jar. Anytime, you negotiate you put the object in the "Compromise" bucket. If you say, "No", you put an object in that one. Hopefully, you have a lot more tokens in the "Yes" bucket. This is a great way for caretakers and parents to have a visualization to make sure you give lots of "Yes" responses as well. My recommendation is for you to aim for the following percentages in each jar. 80% in the Yes Jar, less than 10% in the "No jar", and approximately 10% in the "compromised" jar.

When you do have to say, "no", you can say something like this, "I see a whole bunch in your "Yes" jar, but unfortunately, this is going to have to be put in the "no" jar as there is not a compromise for this one. However, I will continue to give you a lot of "Yes" responses in the future. Does that sound okay?". This is an approach that I have found to be quite effective, but there are not a lot of research studies to support this intervention.

A second proactive strategy that I encourage families of children with defiance to utilize involves the behavioral strategy of "priming". Do you have a child who may have an immediate meltdown after they hear the word "No"? If so, this strategy may be very beneficial to you. I start off and say, "Are you going to stay calm if I say "NO?". Almost always, a "Yes' is said. I then say, "Well great, I will say "Yes". I repeat this type of interaction for approximately 8–10 "yesses" before I change my approach by providing a "No". For example, now, when my child makes a request, I ask, "Are you going to stay calm if I say "No?". I assume your child will say, "Yes". Now, I respond, "I know you want to go right now to your friends' house, but you need to wait for 30 minutes, sound good?". This is what I refer to as a delayed response. In other words, I do not immediately give my child a "no" response but provide a delay for it. By doing this, I am helping my child to be able to better tolerate a future "no" response. I will then repeat this sequence with many more "Yes" responses. When my child asks for something, I continue to use priming by saying something like, "You are going to stay calm if I say "no", right?". Finally, I will provide my child with a "No" response after I use the priming technique of saying, "You are going to stay calm if I say 'no', right?". I will follow it up by saying, "Well, this is a unique situation in which I must say 'no', but I want to thank you for staying calm". All in all, by providing a lot of "Yesses" to your child, it is possible that your child will be able to do a better job of tolerating a "no" response. So put more "Yeses" in your child's piggy bank!

Another proactive strategy is daily exercise. Daily exercise at least 5x/week helps promote better brain functioning and has been found to reduce anger, aggression, hostility, and negative emotions (Shachar *et al.,* 2016). It is possible that if your child is more relaxed and tired from exercise, he may be a bit more happy, tired, and content. Rigorous exercise also can release serotonin in your child's body, which is a neurotransmitter that can help elevate one's mood.

Last but not least, provide your child with <u>lots of choices</u>. Choices can help your child feels he/she has more "control". You can also try to seek for shared control. This means that you give away some control to get some back. For example, when you set a limit, you give back some control/choice. You can say, "You cannot eat the peanut butter sandwich because I already made tacos. But would you like to eat corn, green beans, or some carrots instead?"

Response Strategies

It is critical to have a calm and empathetic response to defiance and meltdowns. It can help to diffuse the tension in the moment for your child if you seek to listen and show understanding and empathy for your child's concern. My best suggestion for you is to stay calm, cool, and collected. Try not to show a reaction or engage in power/control battles. The moment you seek to show disapproval for your defiance or meltdown by making comments such as "That is not okay!", you run the risk of keeping your child in a state of dysregulation. By showing initial empathy, you are helping your child move from their reactive limbic system of their brain to their thinking part of their brain. Remember, our kids cannot think when they are in a state of fear.

When dealing with meltdowns, the goal is to create a world where the emotional need of your child in foster care is met with empathy, understanding, and patience allowing your child to thrive.

Here is a scenario in regard to how you can respond to defiant behavior:

PARENT	Can you please be sure to do your homework now?
CHILD	No, I don't have to, and you can't make me!
PARENT	So true! You are right. I cannot make you. So, you don't want to do it now? Why is that?
CHILD	It's boring and I just don't have to, so just leave me alone!
PARENT	I hear your frustrations. I remember not always liking to do homework. Would you like a little break before you start your homework?
CHILD	Yes

PARENT	Well, how about you ask me if you can start it later?
CHILD	Can I just do it later?
PARENT	Okay, when will you start it?
CHILD	Maybe 6 pm.
PARENT	Well, we are eating at 6 pm. How about you shoot for 5 pm so you can finish it before dinner?
CHILD	Okay.
PARENT	Great job negotiating. You may become an attorney someday because you are so good at it!

Lessons Learned

1. Use priming to remind your child ahead of time of the expectation for how you expect them to behave. Seek acknowledgment from your foster/adoptive child with their intentions to stay calm, even if something unexpected occurs.
2. Your foster/adoptive child will need to have a lot of "Yesses" in their piggy bank to accept a "no". The "Yes" helps to build attachment. When possible, say, "Yes" more often.
3. See a need and meet a need! This is a great way to help avoid a meltdown.
4. Reinforce and encourage your child to engage in the replacement behavior for asking for help, taking a break, or even negotiating as compared to defiant behavior.
5. Don't forget that choices can help to reduce defiant and oppositional behavior.
6. Expect and give room for defiant behavior at times. This way you will be less likely to overreact when it does occur.

References

Greene, R.W. (1998). *The Explosive Child: A New Approach for Understanding and Parenting Easily Frustrated, "Chronically Inflexible" Children*. HarperCollins Publishers.

Shachar, K., Ronen-Rosenbaum, T., Rosenbaum, M., Orkibi, H., & Hamama, L. (2016). Reducing Child Aggression Through Sports Intervention: the Role of Self-Control Skills and Emotions. *Child. Youth Serv. Rev.* 71, 241–249. https://doi.org/10.1016/j.childyouth.2016.11.012

Disrespect   **15**

When our kids are disrespectful, often, we, as parents, respond back with some type of controlling response. Unfortunately, our attempts to "control" a dysregulated and disrespectful child will result in a massive tornado of additional behaviors and challenges.

Disrespectful behavior such as talking back, profanity, and showing rudeness can be very challenging for foster and adoptive parents. Testing boundaries and testing the limits of disrespect is a part of growing up. All kids and teens do it. If you are feeling frustrated with the amount of disrespect that is leashed out, you are not alone. With any feeling of defeat or frustration you may experience as a parent, there is hope! Addressing disrespectful behavior effectively can be a crucial way to foster a harmonious environment.

Research shows that disrespectful children are likely to become rude adults, so it is important to address it with your child/teen (Hafen *et al.*, 2015).

It's a balance of structure and nurture. You cannot just provide only nurture without structure. Disrespectful behavior may need to be ignored in the moment, but, indeed, it needs to be addressed.

Let's explore some of the reasons why children are disrespectful. The main reason is that they have not learned more effective strategies to communicate their frustration. Often, anger, frustration, fear, and feeling misunderstood proceed with disrespectful behavior. Your adopted child

DOI: 10.4324/9781003601081-20

may have not yet learned more effective ways to deal with the emotion in effective ways. As a result, disrespectful words/actions come to the surface. Second, let's be honest: disrespectful words tend to get a big reaction. Our kids learn that is can push our buttons based upon our reactions.

When a child with a trauma history feels something is unfair, they will automatically seek to get something back to gain a sense of control back.

Our kids can learn that they can gain a reaction from us by unleashing a volcano of disrespect. Our signs of disapproval after our children are disrespectful can become quite a predictable way to control us!

Therefore, our reactions often maintain our child's disrespect. Therefore, disrespect can serve as a function of negative attention. Thirdly, disrespect can reflect our child's insecurity and low self-esteem. I call it "leveling" when someone makes a mean comment to another person. It can be effective but socially unacceptable way to temporary make yourself feel better. If I call you stupid, then that assumes that I am not stupid. Furthermore, If I am critical about myself, it will likely result in me being critical about the world and other people, so disrespect can be a natural outpouring of your child's insecurity and self-esteem as well.

Disrespect may serve a few functions (purposes) depending on the context. I will assume there may be two different functions of their disrespect: escape and attention (i.e., as a form of communication).

Sometimes, our children can gain escape from their own fear or other emotions such as frustration or anger (even if temporarily) by means of disrespect. If I am fearful, I can lash out toward someone else and then can temporarily escape the temporary uncomfortable emotions I am experiencing. Perhaps, if your child uses profanity, they have an internal uncomfortable feeling of frustration or anxiety they are trying to remove. When they use profanity, the anxiety and frustration seem to diminish. Unfortunately, it is not the best way to deal with anxiety and frustration, but it can be an effective.

On the other hand, some children engage in disrespect to communicate their frustration, hurt, or fear. I will put this function as attention as they are trying to get their foster/adoptive parents, peers' attention, or their siblings' attention. Your child may become aware of your triggers, and they wisely figure out they can push this button (i.e., your trigger). Boom, they get a reaction! For the rest of this chapter, I will assume that the function of the behavior is a form of communication or protest, likely in the form of attention they receive from their communication.

As you know, we have three ways to change the behavior:

1. Teaching strategies help teach new replacement behaviors.
2. Proactive strategies to seek to avoid the behavior from occurring.
3. Response strategies are the ways we respond to the behavior after it occurs.

Teaching Strategies

When your child uses disrespectful words toward you, it is often an expression of their anger, hurt, frustration, or fear. It is a form of communication, likely that come in the form of attention, even if it is negative attention. Perhaps, the best replacement behavior for disrespectful communication is to teach your foster/adoptive child to engage in more effective communication. Children and teens need to learn how to communicate their frustrations in a safe and non-threatening way. As a trauma-informed foster parent (TIFP), you will be a safe listener as your child shares their frustration with you. Remember, we can provide alternative ways for your child to find their release.

If your child uses disrespect to release their frustration or find escape from an internal frustration, it is important to teach alternative ways for your child to find that release such as using coping strategies. Rigorous exercises such as high-intensity burpees or pushups can be a great outlet. Teaching your child to go take a walk or a jog outside may be an effective strategy to help your child release/escape their frustration in a positive way.

Perhaps, your child can learn to do a squeeze technique where they tense their entire body and then slowly exhale out their mouth. Furthermore, it can be helpful for your child to visualize their frustration leaving their body as they exhale out their mouth. Some children may find some other outlet such as drawing, journaling, or engaging in a hobby as a beneficial way to release their frustrations as well.

Proactive Strategies

Priming can be a good proactive strategy for disrespect that is maintained by attention. For example, let's say you anticipate that your child will be disrespectful when you ask her to show you that she has completed her homework. You can set the stage up and say, "I am going to check to make sure you get your homework done by 5 pm. I know you don't like me looking at your work. However, I think and trust you are going to be respectful this time. I really appreciate your effort!" Priming sets your child up for success by providing expectations of the behaviors you hope to see (before they occur).

Providing frequent choices can be a great proactive strategy, especially when you think your child may back-talk to you or show disrespect. For example, you can say, "We are going to have to stop the video games in 10 minutes, would you rather watch television, hang out with your next-door neighbor, read a book, or do chores?" I like to put one in there that I know they will not choose (i.e., chores) just to make it seem much better. By providing choices, your child may be less likely to be disrespectful.

Another proactive strategy is to keep your expectations clear. It will be a good idea for you to have a family rule where respect is expected! All in all, modeling a culture of respect in your family is beneficial. However, don't forget that your role as a foster/adoptive parent is to spend more time teaching love as compared to teaching rules!

Response Strategies

As a TIFP, try to remember to not take things personally. It is possible the disrespect is simply displaced upon you as their foster/adoptive parent. Take a deep breath. It will pass!

Disrespect to gain attention

If you believe the function of the disrespect is a form of communication to gain your attention, the best response strategy at the point of frustration is to make empathetic statements such as "I see you are really upset" or "I understand you are really mad at me right now". The goal will be to help to disengage the reactive limbic system of your foster/adoptive child, and then you can process with your child how they possibly could have responded in a more appropriate manner. In addition, you can help facilitate a "re-do" with your child by practicing an alternative response. In any case, it is hard, but try to initially respond to disrespect by listening to your child's frustration and making an empathetic comment such as, "I see you are really frustrated with me because I asked you to your homework." It is important to always model respectful behavior to your child, especially when they are disrespectful to you. Therefore, the key will be to validate their feelings in the moment without addressing the profane behavior (in the moment). Your child in foster care is likely operating from the limbic system of their brain if there are high levels of frustration, so It will be best to do a delayed approach and processing the vulgar language later when the child can think and process things.

Another response strategy is to make a when/then statement. The idea is that you tell your foster/adoptive child what you will do when they do a particular behavior. For example, you can simply say, "When you lower your voice volume, then I will be glad to respond to you".

If the function of the behavior is to gain your negative attention, then your child is likely trying to engage you. In this case, it is fine and even encouraged to simply <u>ignore</u> (but only temporarily). At that point, you can use the "when/then" statement ("When you use respectful words, I can then try to help address your concern"). If you believe your child is trying to get that reaction, just let it pass. You may just ignore your child if they roll their eyes at you, it may be better to just ignore it as compared to engage in a lengthy discussion about it. If you do this approach, it will be important at other times to help your child/teen learn new strategies of communication with you. Ignoring the disrespect is only a temporary response and it can be addressed at another time when the frustration is not still at hand.

On the other hand, if you allow yourself to be a pushover and allow your child to be disrespectful to you without ever <u>addressing it</u>, your child will learn that it is okay to be disrespectful to others. If eye-rolling becomes a common situation, you may want to in a calm way respond by saying something like, "I see that you rolled your eyes at me. I just want you to be aware of that as that comes across as disrespectful". Let's practice another way to communicate by saying, "I am really mad at you right now". You can then have them practice saying that to you. Yes, it takes a lot of repetition!

Another strategy you may consider is to respond with some type of silly disarming comment that does not make sense like, "No thanks, I just ate a banana.". This type of response sometimes can disarm your child or even get a laugh in the situation.

Disrespect to gain escape

If the function of the behavior is to release their frustration at the moment, you can find out if there is a way to help support your child. You may find it beneficial to ask your child, "Perhaps, I can help you release your frustration in a different way?". One time, my son was really frustrated at me and was being disrespectful. I asked him if he would like to go outside and crack an egg on my head. Well, both of my kids decided to join in the fun and they both cracked eggs on my head. They were able to release their frustration in a fun way and I was able to connect with them in the moment as we all were laughing in the process. Win Win!!!!

If you have a younger child who uses profanity, you may want to consider using an approach that I refer to as the "alternative lcoation" approach. In this apporach, you encourage your child to go into a room…. such as the bathroom and you can give your child permission to use profanity if they want if they promise to not use profanity when they leave the room. This behavioral strategy is to try to restrict the behavior to one setting, so they learn to engage in that behavior in only one setting.

When your child harms a sibling or someone with disrespectful words, it may be appropriate for you to plan on restitution. Restitution involves doing something nice to the person you just were disrespectful to you. Sometimes, I have my son or daughter say three nice things about the person they disrespected.

There is a great children's book called "How full is your bucket" by Rath *et al.* (2004). This book encourages the readers to be aware that everyone has a bucket, and we need to make sure their buckets are full, especially if you take from their bucket. Therefore, if you take from someone's bucket, you can find a way to put back what you took from them. Perhaps, you can have your child make the bed of their sibling after they made a mean comment to help put it back in their bucket.

Here is a situation that occurred with me:

CHILD   You are so stupid!
ME   (Raising voice) Don't talk to me like!
CHILD   Well, it is true!

ME	Okay, but I do not deserve that, so please stop!!! (Getting more frustrated)
CHILD:	Who?
ME:	Huh?
CHILD:	Who cares!

I must give credit to my child by being funny in the process while using their own disarming technique when I was losing my own cool. However, I certainly did not handle this in the right way by raising my voice.

Here is a way in which I should have responded:

CHILD	You are so stupid!
ME	You seem to be mad at me. Is that because I will not allow your friend to come over!
CHILD	Yes, you are so mean!
ME	I understand how you must be really upset at me. Unfortunately, I have plans for this afternoon and cannot do this. I would really like your friend to come over on another day because I know this is important to you. Would you like that?
CHILD	Yes, can your friend come over tomorrow?
ME	You bet! I think that is a great idea! Let me ask you a quick question. When you said, I was stupid, is there any other way you could have been more respectful?
CHILD	I guess I could have told you I was mad at you for not allowing your friend to come over.
ME	Yes, I think that would have been much better. Good thinking. Would you like me to take you and your friend to get some ice cream tomorrow after you do your homework with your friend?
CHILD	Yeah, that sounds fun!

The result: You have more ownership with your child, and they likely will be more satisfied. In addition, you have maintained positive interactions resulting in a connected approach. Win, win!!

I

It does not always go that smoothly, but hopefully, you get the idea on how not to take the bait with your child when they are disrespectful and to focus on what and how they could communicate that frustration in a better way in the future. Anytime, your child tells you they are frustrated, you also want to be very attentive and encourage their expression as well.

Lessons Learned

1. It is not effective to demand respect.
2. It is best to do a lot of redo's, model respect, and help teach new skills of communicating when your children are disrespectful to you or others.
3. Don't take things so personally. Otherwise, your child may learn to push your buttons to get a reaction out of you.
4. Be sure to catch your child when they show respect and memorialize their success!

References

Hafen, C.A., Allen, J. P., Schad, M. M., & Hessel, E.T. (2015). Conflicts With Friends, Relationship, Blindness, and the Pathway to Adult Disagreeableness. *Pers Individ Dif*. 81, 7–12. https://doi.org/10.1016/j.paid.2015.01.023.

Rath, T., & Clifton, D.O. (2004). *How Full Is Your Bucket*. Gallup Press: New York.

Lying   16

I have dealt with all kinds of behaviors (almost everything that can be horribly imagined in a nightmare); however, the two that seem to get me the most are lying and profanity/vulgar language. In talking to so many foster/adoptive parents, I have found lying, stealing, and hoarding to be the most common problems reported by foster and adoptive parents.

Everyone lies! Unfortunately, it is a normal behavior. In fact, some of us are better at it than others. We all do it at times, and we can only learn to be honest individuals by learning to experiment with those nasty lies. Therefore, it is important to normalize your child's lying behaviors rather than taking things so personally when your child lies to you or others. I am a recovering childhood liar! You are a recovering childhood liar! We need to normalize the lie! I did not say that you accept the lie and become passive about, but we should seek to normalize it.

Okay, take a deep breath and let's dive five feet deeper. It's even more normal for foster kids/adoptive kids to lie. In fact, lying is a part of child and teen development. Many three-year-old children learn to lie in many different types of social situations, and the research shows that as a child age, he/she le (Evans & Lee, 2013). There is a normal part of development that all children go through where young children in this age group share pretend stories and tell tall tales. Sometimes, it may be just fun for them. However, if they do not reach normal development, they may deal with this kind of lies as a 10 or 11-year-old.

If it is so normal, why is it so hard as foster/adoptive parents to respond to our child's lying behavior? First, we have the tendency to project our own fears of our child's future based upon a single lie. Within a split second of one of my children lying to me, I have the tendency to panic. I envision a lifetime of my child lying to people, creating havoc in relationships, getting fired from jobs, and ending up in prison! I often have this

DOI: 10.4324/9781003601081-21

type of internal dialog with myself. "Oh my gosh, he/she is going to end up in prison for the rest of his/her life. He/she continues to tell all these lies. My child steals things, lies about it, and then does not take responsibility for his/her actions. After all this, my child gets mad at me in the process and blames me". In my mind, I tend to exaggerate the significance of one lie, and I am projecting my own fears of what could be because of this one lie. I know I am not alone. It is difficult for foster parents to respond to lying due to our own fear and projection of the future.

The second reason it is hard to deal with is that we desperately want to trust our foster kids. When we can trust them, we can give them more responsibility. Therefore, when our children lie to us, it results in broken trust. This hurts.

The third reason is that it is hard for us to understand why our kids may lie over the most trivial things. I was not a perfect child growing up and recall lying at times, but not nearly as frequently as my kids lie. It is hard for me to relate. In addition, I tend to get more worked up where I envision a future lifelong problem. After all, I eagerly want to trust my own children, but it becomes very hard at times.

To understand why it is so easy for a child with a trauma history to lie, it will be beneficial for us to tap into the field of neuroscience. If in your early years, you have a lot of fear or trauma, the amygdala, and the limbic system (the part of the brain that reacts to quick emotional responses) can have a type of developmental damage that can affect how we feel, perceive, and behave as an adult. I like to think of someone who has a lot of trauma and neglect as having a heightened limbic system, always on guard! The limbic system is our survival center. For many of our kids with a history of neglect and trauma, their limbic system is in a constant state of fear. It becomes hyperaroused/hypersensitive to perceived threat.

A child with a trauma history is more likely to lie when they are in a state of fear. Furthermore, they are more likely to hide the truth if they feel that an adult will be disappointed in them. Also, they are more likely to be deceptive when they believe they will get in trouble. Finally, many kids with trauma histories have deep-rooted shame. Some children feel that they are "bad kids" as they always feel they are getting in trouble. This type of shame is very overwhelming for any child or adult! Therefore, when some children lie, they may be lying to escape the uncomfortable feelings of shame or what they perceive will be the disappointment that will follow from their caretaker.

All in all, when a child is operating in their limbic system, there is a greater chance that a lie will be in the making! Anxiety is uncomfortable, and we all know how much easier it is to get rid of the anxiety through a lie. In these cases, lying serves the function of escape. The child is trying to escape your disappointment, escape the trouble, escape the fear. In addition, many children with trauma histories have a very poor self-image of themselves. They may be less likely to tell the truth if it means that they reveals just another "flaw" that would intensify their feeling of rejection. Therefore, some kids may lie to try to avoid the belief that they may be rejected.

When their limbic system is activated, your child's thinking part of their brain is short circuited. They are not thinking about cause and effect. They will be more concerned about safety in the moment. Their rational, thinking part of the brain (the prefrontal lobe) is not fully in operation. They are only concerned about the moment.

Your child is likely not thinking, if I lie, it will cause more trouble for me. The limbic system operates in the moment and very quickly without thinking! That is why the typical response of a child when asked why they did that is, "I don't know!" They really don't know because they were not thinking in the moment when fear was in operation.

Before we look to some practical suggestions on how to respond to lying behavior, we must first determine what the function or purpose the lying behavior serves. The function of lying behavior likely serves one of the following functions:

1. To get them out of trouble. This is known as an escape function. They also may be escaping an uncomfortable feeling such as shame or the disappointment of their caregiver.
2. To gain access to something they would normally not be able to have. This is known as the access function
3. To gain approval and acceptance from others. This is known as the attention function.

LYING – Escape Function

When talking to many children residing in foster care, they will often tell me that they lie because they want to avoid getting in trouble or they lie to escape their shame. They want to escape their anticipation of what will come when they tell the truth. Therefore, this tells me that fear may likely proceed the lie for many of our kids. Lying to get out of trouble and lying to avoid punishment are two sides of the same coin.

I strongly urge you to never get your child in trouble for telling the truth if you want to decrease the lying behavior. For example, if you ground them from eating candy for the next two weeks when they voluntarily tell you on their own that they ate the candy, it only creates a greater motivation to lie to in the future. Children are going to be more likely to lie with strict parents. If your child constantly lies to escape getting in trouble, my suggestion for you is to change the contingency, so they are less likely to get in trouble when they tell the truth.

I want to provide you with two scenarios. The context of both scenarios is that your daughter shares with you that she skipped a class at school to hang out with a friend.

Option One:

PARENT   What??? I can't believe you did this. You know how important it is to attend school. You know better than this, young lady. You have broken all trust with me, and now you are grounded from your video games for two days. Go to your room and think about your behaviors.

Now, in the future, if provided with an opportunity to lie or not tell your parents about skipping school, my guess is that your child will not tell you or lie in the future to avoid getting in trouble or avoid getting the lecture.

Option Two: (Real-life scenario for me)

ME   You shared with me that you skipped school today to hang out with your friend. Thank you for telling me the truth. I am so proud of you that you told me the truth. I also understand how it can be quite tempting to skip class to hang out with your friends. Can you think of what you would do in the future if your friend was really depressed because they broke up with their friend?

MY CHILD   I guess I could ask to talk to my friend about it after class rather than skipping school.

ME   I am proud of you for coming up with that great idea! Let's do that in the future. I really appreciate that next time you will just talk to your friend after school or at lunch as to how they are feeling. By the way, one of your strengths is that you are compassionate to your friends. I love that about you! That is such a great quality to have, but you also need to make sure that your compassion does not result you in skipping classes in the future. Make sense?

In the future, you certainly want to find ways to reinforce your daughter for attending class. You may think that your child is getting away with skipping class, but, hopefully, if you use the positive intervention first, you may not need to remove consequences or punish her.

I have even told my son and daughter something like this before, "I would normally have you write me a paragraph of what you could have done differently, but since you told me the truth, you do not have to write it as long as you can tell me with your words right now what you would do next time in you were put in the same situation". Now, this kind of interaction helps to build attachment with your child and minimizes the risk of distancing yourself from your child who is adopted. At the same time, you are addressing the need by identifying alternative courses of action that can be done in the future. Win!

Teaching strategies (for escape-maintained lies)

Being a trauma-informed adoptive parent does not mean that you will just be all about rainbows and unicorns when it comes to your child's lying behavior. Your child needs to understand that it is not acceptable to lie. At the same time, you are providing your child with ample opportunities to practice skills related to the replacement behaviors.

Your child's lying behavior is a good opportunity to try to discover why your child believes that lying is their only option. Trauma-informed foster/adoptive parents then try to figure out what skills they need to teach.

Does your child feel safe to be able to use their words? How would you respond if your child were to say, "I really don't want to eat the green beans"? when you may expect them to complete their entire plate? The replacement behaviors for escape-maintained lying are to help teach your child how to escape non-preferred activities or expectations by using their words. For example, a child can be taught to say, "Will it be okay if I only eat half 10 green beans today?". If my child says this, I will do whatever I can to try to reinforce the request as they asked respectfully with by using their words and it avoids a power struggle or meltdown. I am also teaching my child how to gain escape in an appropriate manner.

Proactive strategies (for escape-maintained lies)

If fear proceeds the lie, it brings me to the conclusion that <u>safety, connection, and trust</u> are the key proactive strategies to help your child learn to tell the truth. Therefore, a child should not fear that he will be punished for telling the truth. My children know that they will be less likely to be punished when they are honest and confess to doing something they know I will not approve (in contrast to me finding out without them telling me). There are occasions in which I will give less of a penalty and say, "I was going to restrict your cell phone for 1 day but because you told me the truth, you will only lose it for 2 hours". The reason I do is that I want to be a safe person for my kids to confess to things to me. When I am a safe father, my children will be less likely to lie to me.

Another proactive strategy is to set an environment where you <u>ask for your child's opinion</u>. A child needs to learn that their voice and opinion is important. Some children may learn to lie because they may not have learned the skill of communicating their opinion when it may differ from what others may have.

Another proactive strategy involves being wise about how you approach your child when you have evidence of a shortcoming of your child. In other words, <u>Don't ask a question</u> if you already know the answer to it; instead, <u>make a statement</u>. "I see the cookie crumbs by your bed, can you please go vacuum your room". You can then prompt her how to ask for a cookie with her words.

Now, please put yourself in your child's shoes.

PARENT	Did you take that cookie?
CHILD	(Automatic nervous system activated of child. Limbic System on alert….)
PARENT	(Raising voice) Did you hear me? Did you take that cookie?
CHILD	No!

It becomes easier to understand why a child would lie if cornered by an adult who can get them in trouble. As trauma-informed foster parents, we need to be careful about asking questions that may evoke fear as a result of the activation of the limbic system.

Our questions and statements can be quite triggering to our children:

- "Why did you take that cookie"? – Whoosh Limbic system activated
- "Tell me the truth! You are lying!". BOOM Limbic system activated
- "You are not getting dessert until you fess up". Bam Limbic system activated.

When we respond with a statement/lecture such as, "You are lying to me! You must tell me the truth. How many times have I told you to tell me the truth?" Again, this response will either do one of two things. It may cause your child to just tune you out every time you start to nag, or it also may activate the limbic system based upon their own fear of the situation.

Let's look at another situation.

Option One:

YOU	Did you brush your teeth?
CHILD IN FOSTER CARE	Yes
YOU	No, you didn't! Your toothbrush is not even wet.

Now, let's just stop right there. You set up a situation to give your child in foster care an opportunity to lie. It is as though you were in a police officer role trying to catch her in a crime.

Option Two:

PARENT   "Hey, I see your toothbrush is not wet. Let's go brush your teeth. I will race you. I will give you a five second lead. You brush your and I will brush mine. Remember, you still must brush for 30 seconds. On your mark, set, go!!!"

In option two, the parent did not even give her child in foster care an opportunity to lie. In addition, she made it a fun way to connect with her. Win Win!!!

*It takes positive interactions and positive
relationships to calm a child's reactive stress state.
Furthermore, it takes a lot of repetitions of the
positive interactions to bring healing. Engage in
positive interactions and repeat!*

Response strategies (for escape-maintained lies)

So, how can you respond when your child lies to you? The key is to respond in an empathetic and calm manner. "Hey, I know that fear! I know you may feel the need to hide this, but it is best to tell the truth. We are going to have to work on this, okay?" I urge you to be on the lookout for potential fear for your children. If your foster/adoptive child may be in a state of fear, your primary role is not to lecture, scold, or show signs of disapproval. On the other hand, you want to disarm fear by focusing on empathy, connection, and neutral responses.

In addition, try not to take it personal. If your child lies, you may have thoughts that your child does not respect you or does not care about the truth, but this may simply be that your child is still dealing with their trauma brain and tries to immediately escape situations, which may cause dysregulation as self-protection. If you believe that your child just does not respect you, you will be more likely to react in your own limbic system than to respond deliberately from your prefrontal lobe. Take a deep breath mom or dad, you will get through this!

Lying-Access Function

The second reason your child may lie is because your child believes that the only way to gain a preferred item (such as a toy, money, or a treat) is to lie. Therefore, the function of the behavior is access.

Teaching strategies (for access function)

If the child lies to gain access, our solution would be teaching your child how to gain access to that item in a more appropriate manner. In other words, focus on teaching your child how to ask permission for the pre-ferred item. Your role would be, whenever possible, to provide alternative means for your child to gain access to that item.

Proactive strategies (for access function)

Make sure you provide <u>opportunities for them to access the things</u> that they are more likely to lie about in a more appropriate manner (i.e., access to money, periodic desserts/candy, etc.). You may want to consider allowing your child to have an allowance so they can learn about the value of money and purchase things they want. This may help your child to reduce their lying behavior.

In our household, my kids have always struggled with eating too much ice cream. For this reason, there was a time in the past that I would not buy ice cream because it goes away way too quickly; however, I provided opportunities to go to the ice cream store or Baskin Robbins when it was restricted in the home.

Response strategies (for access function)

Let's provide an example of a hypothetical situation in which your child lies by saying he did not take five cookies out of the cookie jar (when you find the missing cookies in his room by his bed).

First, you do not ask your child if they took the cookies. You simply say something like this:

PARENT	"I see there are cookies on your nightstand. I realize they are really yummy. You may have thought that I would say 'no' if you asked for them. Is that right?"
CHILD	"Yes"
PARENT	"That may be the case, but if I say "no", I will certainly tell you how you could get cookies later. If you would like cookies, what is the best way to get the cookie?"
CHILD	"I could ask for them".
PARENT	"Hey, you got it, champ! Let's practice. How about you ask for me for a cookie".
CHILD	"Can I have 5 cookies"?

PARENT	"I know you want five cookies. I will allow you to have one cookie right now because you asked nicely. And you can have two cookies tomorrow. How does that sound"?
CHILD	"Okay".
PARENT	"Great job asking for the cookies. I will make sure we can have some more tomorrow as well".

If you practice the skill in a redo, you can reinforce the behavior you want to see. In addition, it helps to create a pathway in their brain to learn how to ask again in the future. Win!

Lying-attention function

The third reason why some children lie is that they want to have attention. This attention may be to get attention from you or their peers. Sometimes, foster/adoptive children may even want to create a false reality when their reality is not what they expect. It can be difficult for some children with trauma histories to distinguish fantasy from reality as discussed in chapter two. In a sense, trauma can leave someone so bottled up that it feels safer to hide behind a wall of lies. For example, your child may feel like they fit in or are accepted more by their peers if they make up a wild story about something that happened to them.

Teaching strategies/replacement behaviors

When your child lies to try to gain attention, it is advisable to help your child <u>learn new skills to gain attention from their peers or adults</u> in their lives. Perhaps, you can get your child a joke book and have them learn how to tell jokes to gain attention. You can also teach your child how to gain attention by giving positive comments, smiling, and being kind toward other kids. Hopefully, this will result in your child's peers providing more attention to them in the process.

It is so important for trauma-informed foster parents <u>to provide a lot of praise and positive feedback when they tell the truth</u>. You want to create an environment where your children do not have to fear telling the truth to help overcome those little lies.

Developing an honest and truthful child takes time. Understand, it will take a lot of understanding, a lot of patience, a lot of love, and a lot of safety. It's a marathon not a sprint in aiming for honest, truth-telling children. One lie is not going to make or break it; although, we, as parents, sometimes, think it will.

Proactive strategies

If your child tends to make up crazy stories to gain attention. It may be a good idea to encourage your child and remind your child of their positive traits and their accomplishments on a regular basis. This may help address the need behind the behavior. In addition, it will be good for you to help your foster/adoptive child learn to share their story or how to refuse to tell their story if someone asks.

Another proactive strategy that you can use to help reduce undesirable behavioral (but not expect to eliminate it) is called differential reinforcement of other behavior (DRO). A DRO procedure is simply a way to reinforce the absence of a behavior. You are reinforcing all other behaviors other than the maladaptive behavior (Vladescu & Kodak, 2010; Zane & Davis, 2013).

You can start by taking data to find the average number of lies you catch your child in a day. For example, let's say that your data shows that your child lies on average 12 times per day, which is approximately every 60 minutes. You can take an interval that is less than that like 60 minutes. You provide your child with a sticker if they go 50 minutes without lying. If they lie, you reset the interval and try again. Once they get a certain number of stickers (i.e., ten stickers), they can get a reward or something they would like. Eventually, you will increase the interval when they show success. You may increase the interval that they have to go 100 minutes without lying, then 2 hours, then 3 hours, etc. Eventually when they show success, you can gradually fade out the reward, as we do not want your child to have to depend on a reward. The key is to realize this is a short-term intervention and the reward must be faded out once there is success. This procedure has a lot of empirical support to help reduce behaviors, and it is a positive approach as you are not punishing lying behavior in the process (Vladescu & Kodak, 2010; Zane & Davis, 2013).

You can use a DRO for many different behaviors by reinforcing the absence of the behavior (i.e., in a sense you are reinforcing all other behaviors except lying). I have used this for my own kids and for a lot of my clients for behaviors such as profanity.

Responding strategies

When our child lies, it is best to stay calm and avoid asking why questions.

Focus on progress not perfection! We cannot expect to eliminate lying. Progress is our goal! My response to the lie is usually to attempt to a "re-do". Here is what I want you to remember.

Your primary job as a parent is not to teach them to always tell the truth….it is to love them, no matter what!!!

It is important for everything to be done in the context of love, even when they lie. It is part of a connected, attached relationship that your child will feel safe enough to tell the truth.

Lessons Learned

1. At all costs, avoid nagging and lecturing. Try an empathetic and connected approach. Use your child's lying behavior as an opportunity to build attachment and teach new skills rather than as an opportunity to simply "correct a behavior".
2. Don't ask a "Why" question. You will likely get the response of "I don't know". Furthermore, you probably will not get an answer that appeases your inquiry.
3. Instead of asking your child a question, make a statement like, "I see the wrappers of candy behind your bed. Can you please go pick them up and put them in the trash? Also, let's practice asking for candy right now".

4. Your child should not have to fear telling the truth. If you punish a child for telling you when they break a rule, you may create a situation where they will fear telling you the truth in the future.
5. Expect that your child will lie at times. This is normal. If you have the expectation that your child always will tell you the truth, you will constantly feel discouraged and defeated as a foster/adoptive parent.
6. Be patient. Don't frustrate yourselves for an unreasonable time to learn to tell the truth. It takes time! Remember, we are not in a sprint, but we are in a marathon race with lots of detours. Remember the timing of the teachable moment. Your child cannot be taught the moral lesson of lying based upon one situation. It takes time.
7. Don't take it personally. Their lying behavior is not your fault. As trust develops along with the passing of time, which brings maturity, lying will hopefully decrease. It is likely based upon their past experiences.

References

Evans, A. D. & Lee, K. (2013). Emergence of Lying in Very Young Children. *Developmental Psychology*.

Zane, T. & Davis, C. (2013). Differential Reinforcement Procedures of Other Behavior (DRO). In Volkmar, F. R. (Ed.) *Encyclopedia of Autism Spectrum Disorders*. Springer. https://doi.org/10.1007/978-1-4419-1698-3_1903

Vladescu, J.C., & Kodak, T. (2010). A Review of Recent Studies on Differential Reinforcement During Skill Acquisition in Early Intervention. *J Appl Behav Anal*, 42(2), 351–355.

Hoarding and Stealing **17**

When your foster or adoptive child accumulated and hoards items such as food, toys, random objects, your child may try to be finding security in a world which historically has been chaotic. It can be easy to understand how food or other items could bring a sense of security for that child.

Hoarding

One of the most common behavioral problems we see for foster/adoptive children is hoarding and stealing. Children with a history of neglect may have grown up in an environment with inadequate food. When this occurs, children do not become accustomed to getting their needs met by adults. Some children with hoarding are operating by innate insecurity of never having enough; therefore, they sometimes will collect food as it can become a sense of security for them. For this chapter, let's assume the primary function of hoarding is to gain access to items or perhaps a type of access to an intangible such as security. Therefore, the key will be to help your child learn how to gain access to food or other items in a more appropriate manner.

It is possible that someone may try to engage in stealing and hoarding behaviors for other functions such as attention; however, gaining access to items is a more common function. We do not want to design an intervention strategy to address stealing or hoarding until we have a better understanding of the function of the behavior.

Many foster/adoptive children will engage in hoarding behaviors because food makes them feel safe. By hoarding food, they do not have to worry if it will be there. This is especially true for children who may have grown up in an oversees orphanage and did not have access to

DOI: 10.4324/9781003601081-22

consistent, healthy meals. However, hoarding behaviors are also seen in children who were survivors of neglect growing up.

Hoarding behavior can meet a type of instinctual need for our foster kids/adoptive kids. When kids have a history of going hungry, they have learned not to trust adults to provide for their needs, so hoarding behavior is a survival behavior.

In fact, it is wise and smart for a child to learn to hoard food, right? I think if we can come to understand this, it allows us as parents to be much more patient, understanding, and empathetic. Also, it is important to know that research shows there may be some genetic predisposition to hoarding.

When they were younger, both my son and daughter have had a history of taking objects that did not belong to them and hoarding items. My son used to store random objects under his pillow (like paper clips, screwdrivers, measuring tapes, plastic forks, and rocks) for the first few years of living with me. However, over time, as attachment developed between my son and I, he slowly started to avoid the hoarding of these items. I also helped to provide a special place where he could put his belongings so no one would take them. I think this behavioral strategy helped him tremendously as he was fearful that someone was going to take his special belongings.

Your child may also find that they find security in food. If they are insecure, they may realize that by having and eating food, it brings security and comfort. You know how many times you have used eating to gain comfort after a long and stressful day?

Stress also can cause many children with histories of trauma to be hungrier. The reason is that stress impacts the blood sugar levels in our blood. Therefore, it is so important to make sure our foster/adoptive kids have regular and consistent meals and snacks. Aim to make sure your child gets something in their stomach at least once every 3 hours.

When Andrew and Kayla first arrived in my home, I was quite surprised to see how much food they put on their plate, especially at buffets. They always wanted a whole bunch on their plate, even if they did not eat it all. My response was to say, "You can have some more after you eat the first plate, but let's just put a little less on your plate now". In addition, I noticed my child would bring random things to bed with them (tape measurer, screwdrivers, forks, paperclips, etc.). This likely provided my child with a certain amount of security. When my child was at a previous foster home, there were many other kids in the home, and my child did not have as many personal belongings. Therefore, my child wanted to keep things with them as a form of safety. As Andrew and Kayla both felt safer with me, their hoarding behaviors decreased over time.

Some foster and adoptive children hoard as they struggle in developing relationships with people, so they resort to trying to find a type of false identity or relationship with objects. In addition, some children develop a sense of attachment to the object, so it can be a difficult decision to determine which objects they should keep or throw away. I have met some children who felt like the objects had feelings, so they did not want to hurt the feelings of the object by discarding it.

There are teaching strategies, proactive strategies, and responding strategies to help reduce hoarding behavior. I am going to assume the function of the hoarding behavior is access (that may be access to an item or access to comfort). Therefore, the replacement behavior will be to teach your child to ask for the food. This means when your child asks for food, we want to be able to say "yes" whenever possible. Obviously, you cannot always say "yes", so we will discuss how to respond when your child eats too much or the wrong kind of foods as well.

Teaching strategies

If the function of hoarding behavior is to gain access to items, the replacement behaviors and teaching can be used to help your child learn how to gain access to those items in more appropriate way. In my professional practice, I will often do role plays with foster and adoptive children by having them practice asking for food or items. In addition, they can learn to ask for a special place to put some of their time (like a drawer). Be playful and fun in working with your foster/adoptive child on how to ask for food or other items.

Proactive strategies

These strategies are things you can do to avoid your foster/adoptive child from hoarding food.

1. *Noncontingent Access*
    This behavioral strategy is to allow free access to certain food at any time. By theory, if they have free access to certain nutritious foods, we will hope that the hoarding behavior would decrease. You can

keep a drawer that is their own drawer in the kitchen or even in your child's bedroom. You can place apples, bananas, oranges, nuts, protein bars, etc., in the cabinet.

2. *Color-Coded Restricted Access*

   If you do not want to provide noncontingent access, you can develop a code where you put a "Red" color on the cabinet when it is restricted and a "Green" color when it is available. You can then put items in the cabinet that they can eat. This may be good for a child who tends to overeat in an unhealthy manner and provides a visual for them to understand so they do not repetitively ask you.

3. *Prearranged Food Items (without replacement)*

   You may put non-nutritious items in the cabinet with appropriate portions. Perhaps, you can put 20 chips in a container in the cabinet. Your child can choose to eat that, but once it is gone, it is gone for the rest of the day.

4. Make sure you have consistent, healthy meals with healthy snacks in between.

5. Reinforce your child when they eat slowly. It takes your brain 20 minutes to register that it is full, even though you are already full. This is how it becomes much easier to overeat when you eat fast. You may want to try to encourage your child to eat their food with chopsticks. If your child is not used to eating with chopsticks, it will likely slow down the time between bites.

6. If your child tends to want to eat a lot of unhealthy foods, you can encourage your child to eat something healthy in between. For example, if your child eats a bowl of cereal and wants a second bowl of cereal, you can then encourage your child to eat an apple first and then provide your child with another bowl of cereal with a reduced portion.

7. Most ADHD medications suppress appetite. If your child has ADHD and is medicated with a stimulant, you will want to make sure you understand that the time-release pills will likely wear out soon after they arrive home from school. Be proactive and get ready to offer snacks frequently, as when the medication wears out, your foster/adoptive child may get hungry quickly.

8. Allow your foster or adoptive child to be involved in the decision items of which items to discard or keep. For example, if they have 30 items, you can tell them they can keep 20 items, and then allow them to decide which items they can keep and which ones to discard. You can implement a "One in, one Out" rule where they can

keep one item and discard of the other item. This is a good way to help provide a limit on the acquisition of new items and to help your child to become more comfortable in throwing some items in the trash.

Responding strategies

It is best to avoid punishing hoarding behavior. If we punish a child for hoarding, it may lead to shame. In addition, punishment does not teach the new behavior that trauma-informed foster parents are seeking to address. If your adoptive child hoards food, I suggest you remind them that they can have more food later. As you know, you want to be gentle, calm, and reassuring. Often, children with a history of neglect and trauma may take larger portions of food than needed, which is like hoarding. As mentioned before, it takes your body 20 minutes to realize it is full after eating. One great strategy is to allow your child to have one helping. If your child wants seconds, you can say, "You are welcome to have more, but let's wait 20 minutes to see if you are still hungry then". Often, once they are away from the kitchen table and doing an activity, they may not eat as much for their second helping. This strategy can be quite effective to help reduce the amount your child eats.

Stealing Behavior

Stealing behavior can be especially alarming for foster and adoptive parents. It is essential to address the stealing behavior promptly to effectively prevent it from becoming a persistent problem. When a child steals items, I am assuming that most of the time it is to gain access to items that they do not believe they would otherwise be able to obtain. However, it is possible that there could be other functions such as attention or sensory (related to the feelings of adrenaline rush that occurs in their body).

There are several reasons why foster/adoptive children tend to steal. First, many foster kids do not trust that their caretakers will provide for their own needs, so they learn to take matters into their own hands (literally) by stealing. Second, stealing can give some children a sense of control in their lives. Third, stealing can be used as a coping mechanism to deal with feelings of sadness and anxiety. Finally, stealing may bring security for a child who may not have had certain items in the past.

Within the first month of living with me, I caught my children stealing small items from stores. This was a bit unexpected and shocking to me at first. However, as I reflected upon my children's history, it became more understanding of how stealing helped to fulfill some unmet needs for my children.

Teaching strategy

I am assuming the function of the behavior is access. Therefore, the teaching strategy will be to help your foster/adoptive child learn how to ask for a particular item. If they cannot get the item, you can teach them how to negotiate by asking what they can do to earn the item in the future. Perhaps, you can do role plays with your child in foster care, so they practice the behavior you want them to do.

Proactive strategies

There are several proactive strategies that you can use to help avoid or prevent stealing (based upon the function of access).

1. If your child is stealing money/items, you want to make sure they can gain access to money/other items by other means (allowance, chores, etc.). This is important as it teaches the value of money. They will likely continue to steal money if they are not able to get money by other means.
2. You can also use a DRO procedure. That is, you set a period that you give your child money if they do not steal the money/item. For example, if you go 4 days without taking money, I will give it to you. Sometimes, the site of money becomes a discriminative stimulus for stealing it. You can help break the site of money as a cue to stealing by placing some money in various places in your home. You can tell your child that they will get the money if they do not take it after a specified period. I suggest that you remind your child that you will be placing money in open areas for a short period of time (maybe a few hours), then if they do not take it, they get it. You can then try to

increase the amount of time that the money will be out in the open from a few hours to several hours.

3. Encourage and model gratitude for your children. It may be beneficial for you to try to help your child to be thankful for what they have rather than for what they do not have. You may even want to have your child keep a "gratitude journal" to foster a sense of appreciation.

Responding strategies

If your foster/adoptive child steals an item from a store or someone else, it will be important for you to help your child take responsibility. There have been many occasions where we have had to go back into a store to return a candy bar, gum, or some other item that was taken. This is good as a natural consequence to their action. Don't forget to speak calmly. Lectures are likely not as effective as teaching them an alternative way to get their need met.

Lessons Learned

1. Provide opportunities for your child to earn money to buy things for themselves. This may help your child's need to steal.
2. Provide a cabinet of food for your child that has healthy snacks that they can have at any time.
3. Help your child take responsibility when they do steal by returning the item to the owner/store.
4. Model the value of the blessings of giving over receiving. Instead of throwing away old toys or items, have your child be involved in helping to give some of their belonging to other needy children. Modeling a giving heart is an important value for your children to learn, which may help them to be more considerate for the needs of others.

Digital Addiction **18**

> One of the best gifts you can give yourself and your foster/adoptive child is to periodically disconnect from your devices and truly connect with your child.

In the age of technology, social media, screen time, and gaming have become an integral part of everyday life for our youth. As we continue to advance technologically, children and adolescents are increasingly exposed to screens in various forms: smartphones, tablets, television, and gaming consoles. These devices can be incredible access to information and social information, we are seeing more and more youth and adults become addicted to their devices.

Many teens are becoming addicted to Snapchat, Instagram, Discord, Twitter, YouTube, and other social media platforms. These platforms are habit forming and are designed to engage the youth to spend longer times on social media to stay connected to their peers. May older children and teens are constantly engaged on their cell phones and devices due to their fear of missing out (FOMO). Also, many of our foster kids who become addicted to their devices come to expect instant gratification. The user expects an instant response with messaging apps, and this constant feedback reinforces the need to stay engaged. The COVID-19 pandemic increased the reliance upon screens due to remote learning and the inability to connect with their peers in person.

There is a physiological component to digital addiction with our brain's reward system. Dopamine is a neurotransmitter associated with pleasure. Every time an individual engages in a rewarding activity such as access to social media or gaming dopamine is released.

The repetitive engagement in these activities can lead to a conditioning of the brain, where the individual associates screen time and feelings of pleasure as a reward. In addition, other activities such as exercise,

DOI: 10.4324/9781003601081-23

connecting with family, focusing on schoolwork, and interacting with family become less rewarding.

Unfortunately, over time, the brain can be desensitized so that more screen time or games are needed to receive the same level of pleasure. This can lead to compulsive, habit-forming behaviors and addictions. This type of addiction can be difficult because it is reinforced both psychologically and physiologically.

Digital or Technology addiction which refers to when an individual becomes addicted to devices including cell phones, tablets, and online platforms to access social media. This results in compulsive and almost uncontrollable reliance upon digital devices and screens to the detriment of other activities such as school, exercise, developing other hobbies, and face-to-face socialization.

Anderson *et al.* (2018) found that 45% of teens are online "almost constantly" (p. 2). These researchers showed that the study in 2018 was almost double as to what was reported in their 2014 study (p. 8). In the same study, 85% of teens reported they have access to a gaming console at home, and 97% of teens acknowledged that they play video games (p. 9).

In addition, children in foster care are especially prone to developing gaming and digital addictions. So how much is too much gaming? That's a great question, and one that does not have an easy response. It may be easy to see how 5–6 hours of video games/media time on a regular basis is not healthy for a child; however, it may be a healthy, therapeutic release for a child to play 2–3 hours on a weekend after they have just interacted with their peers, engaged in a sports activity and completed all their homework. In 2023, the American Academy of Pediatrics updated their recommendations from 2016. In 2016, the recommendation by AAP was that children and teens should have no more than 2 hours of screen time for children. However, in 2023, the new recommendations removed the amount of screen time by providing general guidelines of video usage (AAP, 2023).

The American Psychiatric Association is considering adding a new disorder called "Internet Gaming Disorder" into the diagnostic manual. If this does occur, individuals who have at least five of the following characteristics will have an "Internet Gaming Disorder" (APA, p. 795).

1. Preoccupation: Thinking about video games frequently, even when not playing.
2. Withdrawal: Feeling restless when not playing.
3. Tolerance: A need to play more games or more power games to maintain excitement.

4.   Reduce: Failure of attempts to reduce video gaming.
5.   Giving Up Other Activities: A reduction of other activities.
6.   Continue despite problems: Continued dependence on gaming, despite the problems associated with gaming.
7.   Deception: Lies about the amount of gaming.
8.   Escape mood: Plays games to reduce or escape stress.
9.   Risk: Risks the loss of relationships or employment due to gaming.

This definition is not without controversy. Some argue that many gamers are psychologically well-adjusted, but they may meet at least five of these characteristics and be falsely labeled as having a problem. Whether or not one can consider excessive gaming a type of disorder that should be included in the diagnostic manual is debatable; however, excessive gaming is not healthy if it interferes with relationships and functioning levels.

There are a host of physical and emotional symptoms associated with excessive gaming and digital devices. Here are a few of them:

1.   Increased gaming can equate to decreased face-to-face social interaction. Although some gamers argue that they get increased socialization with Role Play Games (RPGs), the interactions are not the same as face-to-face interactions.
2.   Increased gaming may lead to decreased ability to concentrate. It can also lead to decreased motivation to do other activities that do not have as much sensory input (i.e., reading, exercise, etc.). Often, individuals who spend excessive time on video games are not motivated to do other activities.
3.   Some people use video games to escape the pressures in "real life" world. They then do not learn how to use other coping strategies to cope. Screen time offers an easy escape from real-world stress and negative emotions. Many foster/adoptive children turn to their devices to avoid dealing with challenging emotions and situations. When an individual is reinforced by avoiding or escaping stress and pressure, it can be a reinforcing type of loop that results in over-reliance upon the digital platform.
4.   Increased television watching, and gaming has been associated with decreased academic performance (Adelantado-Renau et al., 2019).
5.   Increased gaming may lead to increased health risks and concerns related to sedentary life. Other concerns such as increased weight gain, increased risk of type 2 diabetes, decreased ability to regulate stress, increased risk for cardiovascular disease, increased risk for anxiety and depression, and increased risk for sleep problems

(Haghjoo *et al.*, 2022; Nakshine *et al.*, 2022). The blue light emitted by screens can decrease the production of melatonin (the hormone that regulates sleep patterns) resulting in a disruption of sleep (Shechter *et al.*, 2018).

6.   Many RPGs have a culture where people can be quite mean-spirited to each other. Many gamers will make unkind remarks to others during games.

On the other side of the coin., video games and media can be positive. If done in moderation, they can be a great stress release. There are some great learning applications out there as well. Gaming can also be done to help bring families together with a healthy sense of fun and healthy competition.

I have seen how excessive preoccupation can affect my own children in both positive and negative ways. On the positive, I have observed how my son would use YouTube videos as a young child to increase his passion on topics including science and weather patterns. Negatively, when I first received my children from another foster home, they were excessively dependent upon video games. One of my children would engage in huge meltdowns when denied access to video games. If allowed, my child would spend endless hours on their tablet. Over the years, I have slowly tried to help my child reduce the amount of time on games as I was seeing how it affected their behaviors. Early after receiving my children, one specific thing that I have done is to create a Wednesday night family night. No video games, YouTube, or video is allowed on Wednesdays. Instead, we play games as a family. When I shared my agenda to have Wednesday Family Night with my children, I was fully expecting a big battle. I was quite surprised that both of my children reacted in a semi-positive way about it.

It is important for trauma-informed foster parents (TIFPs) to provide some healthy and reasonable rules for their children in foster care. Hiniker *et al.* (2016) outlined several rules that parents should utilize with technology and their children. Here are some great rules that all TIFPs should enforce with technology (p. 5).

1.   **Be present**: There are certain situations in which you can restrict access to social media to focus on relationships. For example, no social media while eating dinner together.
2.   **Privacy**: It is important to teach children to not give their personal information out to strangers.

3. **Moderate use**: Technology can be used in moderation. It is important to find balance by engaging in other activities.
4. **Parent audit**: Your child needs to be able to have general privacy, but a random audit of the phone by parents is advisable.
5. **Content restrictions**: Certain games may need to be banned based upon the age of your child. It is important to pay attention to the ratings of the games and do not allow your child in foster care to play games/applications that are beyond the recommended age.
6. **Not while driving**: Drivers should not use their cell phones. Period!
7. **Not at night**: Do not allow cell phone usage past their bedtime.
8. **No hypocrisy**: Parents must live by the rules too!
9. **No sexual content**: No viewing or sending any pornography. There are certain apps applications like Snapchat that allow your child to send a photo that is immediately erased. It is never appropriate to send or receive naked photos.
10. **No bad language**: Profanity and bad language are not allowed on cell phones.
11. **Time-bound**: Create time limits and enforce them. Some apps and settings will shut the game/app off when the time limit has expired.

We know that excessive screen time, social media, and gaming is a huge problem for children, teens, and adults. As you know, there are three ways to change behavior: teaching strategies (to teach a new behavior), proactive strategies (to avoid behavior) and responding strategies. Let's investigate how we can help teach our foster/adoptive child how to learn new skills regarding their social media usage.

Teaching Strategies

Social media, gaming, and screen time is a behaviors that we are not seeking to completely remove from our kids. It is a behavior that we are wanting to help our children learn to manage their behavior, so it does not become excessive. It will likely not be effective to just tell your child to stop playing all their games or stop looking at their cell phone. That will obviously not work, and it will drive both you and your child crazy in the process! You must help your child learn to engage in other activities to replace their screen time. If your child is used to 3-4 hours of video games, it may be difficult to simply tell your child to reduce it to 1 hour of video games each day without proactive planning. What will they do with the other 2 hours? You need to provide activities and other things for your child to do during that time.

It also may be a good idea to encourage your child who is in foster care to play video games in person (rather than online). This may lead to opportunities to change the activity and do something other than just gaming. Also, it is always better for social purposes to do things in person when possible.

Another teaching strategy involves teaching and encouraging your child to self-monitor their own behavior (i.e., recording the actual amount of time gaming). Often, youth are not aware of the amount of time on gaming, so this may help reduce the amount of time, so they are not so dependent on gaming and screen time. Perhaps, you can talk to your child about what they feel is a reasonable amount of screen time and give them a special treat if they meet their personal goal. Many smartphones and devices include features that track screen usage, allowing users to monitor how much time they spend on certain apps. This can help your youth to identify the problem of their increased reliance upon screentime.

Proactive Strategies

Consider putting restrictions on how long your child needs to be on a break before playing more games. For example, for a child who plays 6 hours per day, you may consider a rule that he/she should take a 1-hour break after 1 hour of gaming. You can then increase the amount of the break (i.e., a 2-hour break after 1 hour of gaming), etc.

Monitoring your child's device is critical! For younger children, it is a good idea for you to put passwords on the devices or keep the device or console. Some parents find it helpful to keep the console cords. If need be, you may need to change your wi-fi password and not tell your child the password. For teens, there are applications or setting on your phone that you can add in the parental settings that allow one to restrict the number of minutes that one plays certain games. You can also use the setting that shuts off all the games after a certain time frame. In addition, I strongly encourage you that when you first give your child/teen a cell phone, that you create a rule where they turn in their cell phone into you at a certain time, so it does not interfere with your child's sleep schedule.

Consider limiting notification on your cell phone. Notifications from apps and social media platforms can be highly distracting and encourage individuals to instantly respond. By changing the notification system and teaching your child in foster care that they can devote several times a day to respond to the texts of others. This may be hard to convince your youth to do, but it might be helpful if they can buy into the need to do this.

Take scheduled breaks. I encourage individuals to do the 60–60 rule. After engaging on your device or console for 60 minutes, take a 60-minute break. During this time, they can do other activities. Also, set up a contingency that they are welcome to play their games after they do their homework and chores. As discussed previously, this is considered the Premack contingency. First, do your homework, read for 15 minutes, do their chores, then you do access their gaming consoles and devices. Once they have access to their device, they can then implement the 60–60 rule.

It is also important to help your child stay engaged in other healthy activities. Physical exercise (such as swimming, jumping on the trampoline, riding their bike) and creative hobbies such as painting, writing, drawing, etc., may be good replacement behaviors for your child to engage in. As a psychologist, I encourage families to develop a "Boredom Buster Basket" for their children. The basket can contain a list of ideas of activities to engage in, along with their favorite items such as paint, markers, Legos, etc. This can be helpful for child or teen who struggles with finding other things to do to occupy their time.

Consider periodic long-term fasts from digital platforms. This type of digital detox of intentionally stepping away from screens for a set period of time (a weekend or half a day) can help reset the brain's dopamine reward system and provide your youth with an opportunity to connect with face-to-face relationships. You can use this time to do things together as a family. Creating a Family Night with no screentime and gaming may seem like torture for your child, but if you start this habit early and practice consistently, it will hopefully be developed into a positive and fun ritual.

It is possible for foster parents to monitor the social media sites of their child while still respecting their need for privacy. For example, DeGarmo (2014) encourages foster parents to join the same social network site that their child uses under as well as becoming their "friend" on the social media site. This allows the foster parents to better monitor things and provides a type of extra accountability for the child regarding their posts. However, it is also important to know that our teens are sneaky and still can post inappropriate posts to only select friends.

Response Strategies

Regardless of whether your child engages in excessive social media, and screen time, it is important for you to monitor the type of video games that your child is playing. Do you know the type of chat that your child is being exposed to as well in the game? The Entertainment Software Rating Board (ESRB) posts ratings and guidelines for games that are based upon the age of the player.

All in all, gaming, social media, and screen time can be positive if done in moderation; however, if it interferes with schoolwork, job, relationships, or access to other hobbies or interests, an intervention may need to be developed to help reduce one's dependence on gaming and screen time.

Lessons Learned

1. When you first provide a cell phone or device for your child, create rules and restrictions early on. It is a lot better to start with certain habits then creating a new rule after a problem occurs. It is perfectly reasonable to have a time out zone for cell phones when they go to bed, so utilize apps for cell phone restrictions.
2. Help teach your child to self-monitor their own screen time. Many phones have screentime options which monitor how much time they spend on it. Set goals with each other to not go beyond a specified amount of time. This will be good for you as well!
3. When your child shows trust, provide more privileges. For example, I provided my kids with a cell phone without a data plan at first. Once they showed responsibility, I added a data plan for them.

References

Adelantado-Renau, M., Molier-Urdiales, D., Cavero-Redondo, I., Beltran-Valls, M.R., Martinez-Vizcaino, V., & Alvarez-Bueno, C. (2019). Association Between Screen Media Use and Academic Performance Among Children and Adolescents. *JAMA Pediatr.* 173 (11), 1058–1067.

American Academy of Pediatrics (2023). Screen Time Guidelines. Retrieved from https://www.aap.org/en/patient-care/media-and-children/center-of-excellence-on-social-media-and-youth-mental-health/qa-portal/qa-portal-library/qa-portal-library-questions/screen-time-guidelines/

American Psychiatric Association. (2013). *Diagnostic and Statistical Manual of Mental Disorders* (5th ed.). https://doi.org/10.1176/appi.books.9780890425596.

Anderson, M., Smith, A., & Caiazza, T. (2018). Teens, Social Media & Technology. *Pew Research Center.*

DeGarmo, J. (2014). *Keeping Foster Children Safe Online: Positive Strategies to Prevent Cyberbullying, Inappropriate Contact, and Other Digital Dangers.* Jessica Kingsley Publishers

Hiniker, A., Schoenebeck, S., & Kientz, J. (2016). Not at the Dinner Table: Parent's and Children's Perspectives on Technology Rules. https://doi.org/10.1145/2818048. 2819940.

Haghjoo, P., Siri, G., Soleimani, E., Farhangi, M.A., & Alesaeidi, S. (2022). Screentime Increases Overweight and Obesity Risk Among Adolescents: A Systematic Review and Dose=Response Meta Analysis. *BMC Prim. Care.* 23, 161.

Nakshine, V.S., Thute, P., Khatib, M., & Sarkar, B. (2022). Increased Screen Time as a Cause of Declining Physical, Psychological Health, and Sleep Patterns: A Literary Review. *Cureus,* 14(10). https://doi.org/10.7759/cureus.30051.

Schechter, A., Kim, E.W., St-Onge, M.P., & Westwood, A.J. (2018). Blocking Nocturnal Blue Light for Insomnia: A Randomized Controlled Trial. *J Psychiatr Res.* 196, 202. https://doi.org/10.1016/j.jpsychires.2017.10.015.

Epilogue

It is not easy being a trauma-informed foster parent (TIFP). Parenting a child with trauma along with attachment issues comes with sweat, tears, and feelings that no one can truly understand unless you have been there. If you are anything like me, there have been multiple times that you may wonder if you need to call it quits! Hopefully, this book has encouraged you to keep hope alive. Trauma-informed foster and adoptive parenting is a marathon, not a sprint. When you feel like throwing in the towel, my hope is that you will pause and reflect about taking one day at a time. Try to enjoy the moment in all the blood, sweat, and tears and remind yourself of the small ways you are making a difference in the life of your child. If you do not hear it now from your child, hopefully, when they get older, you will hear from them, "thank you dad/mom for always being there for me".

There is no greater joy than seeing trust develop
between you and your foster or adoptive child.

It may take days, months, or years to get there, and when you hear "mommy" or "daddy" for the first time, it may send shivers down your spine. When your adoptive child continues to trust you with this greatest title, it should not be unnoted.

Trauma can hinder the relationship-building process between you and your child; however, there is hope as you remain steadfast in your goal to provide trauma-informed practices to your child. When your child snuggles up next to you, asks for hugs and kisses, or requests you when they need comfort, it is a sign that your child is beginning the scary process of trusting you.

DOI: 10.4324/9781003601081-24

It can be overwhelming as a foster/adoptive parent to reflect upon the hardships and suffering our kids have endured through the years. It can also be hard as parents to know how to support our kids with their trauma histories. However, I am here to remind you that our kids in their trauma area are also resilient little creatures. Most of our kiddos eventually bounce back, especially when they are surrounded in the right environment.

Although trauma does not make one become stronger, Levine (2010) reminds us that there is a great paradox in trauma.

Trauma has the power to both destroy and weaken, but it also can result in transformation and resurrection.

This power to resurrect can lead children with trauma histories to experience posttraumatic growth. Post-traumatic growth is a term in the positive psychology movement which focuses on how survivors of trauma can eventually find purpose in life. In fact, it can result in an individual developing a better understanding of themselves and the world that would otherwise not have occurred without their unfortunate traumatic experiences (Dell'Osso *et al.*, 2022).

Although we would not with upon trauma for any soul, sometimes good things can come out of bad things! Adversity can result in positive changes when provided with the right nutrients to foster their seed of greatness.

Survivors who persevere through their own trauma can become role models and leaders to others. There is something so sweet about a trauma survivor who bounces back from pain and adversity to be a sweet aroma of positivity to others.

Thank you for embracing the pain of your child and striving to support your child unconditionally with love and empathy for the greater purpose of watching your child heal and thrive overtime. You are a hero!

References

Dell'Osso, L., Lorenzi, P., Nardi, B., Carmassi, C., & Carpita, B. (2022). Post Traumatic Growth (PTG) in the Frame of Traumatic Experiences. *Clin Neuropsychiatry*. 19 (6), 390–393. doi: 10.36131/cnfioritieditore20220606.

Levine, P.A. (2010), *In an Unspoken Voice: How the Body Releases Trauma and Restores Goodness*. North Atlantic Books.

Glossary

Acute trauma A short-term traumatic or stressful event that results in psychological impairment. It is an isolated traumatic event

Adrenaline A hormone in the body also known as epinephrine. This hormone is released when one experiences fear. This hormone is involved with the "flight of fight" stress response and results in increased blood circulation and breathing.

Amygdala This is an almond-shaped part of the brain involved with fear, emotions, and motivation.

Applied Behavior Analysis (ABA) A scientific understanding of behavior that seeks to understand behavior in context of the environment.

Behavioral Momentum A technique used to help children become more compliant by asking the child to do easy tasks first before asking to do a task he/she would more likely refuse.

Cerebrum The cerebrum is the largest part of the brain and consists of the left and right hemispheres of the brain.

Chronic Trauma This kind of trauma is trauma that has been repeated over a long period of time. Chronic trauma is a broad term (as compared to complex trauma) that may include domestic violence, natural disasters, or being repeatedly abused by an individual

Compassion Fatigue Burnout and fatigue often experienced by foster and adoptive parents due to caring for the needs of the children in their care. It is also known as secondary trauma.

Complex Trauma This kind of trauma is repeated trauma that occurs directed toward a child by a caretaker or parent.

Connecting Strategies Strategies from Trust-Based Relationship Intervention (®) that help disarm fear and help to promote greater attachment between parent and child.

Coregulation A process in which one individual helps another individual to become calm and relaxed.

Correcting Strategies Strategies derived from Trust-Based Relationship Intervention (TBRI®) that are designed to help parents learn how to respond to behaviors from their children.

Cerebral Cortex This is also known as the gray matter of the brain. It is the outer area of the cerebrum

Cortisol This hormone is produced by the adrenal gland. It is also known as a stress hormone as it helps to regulate stress.

Differential Negative Reinforcement of Alternative Behavior (DNRA) An individual is allowed to escape a non-preferred activity or situation based upon completing a specific alternative response.

Differential Reinforcement of Other Behavior (DRO) This approach seeks to reduce a particular maladaptive behavior by reinforcing all other behaviors other than the maladaptive behavior.

Dysregulation A state in which an individual is not able to regulate their emotional response, resulting in mood swings, meltdowns, and behavioral outbursts

Emotional regulation The process to recognize and respond to one's emotions.

Empowering Strategies Strategies from Trust-Based Relationship Intervention (TBRI®) that parents use to help meet the physical and environmental needs of the children under their care.

Fixed Mindset A mindset in which an individual does not believe that they can develop and grow.

Function of Behavior The purpose or reason a behavior continues.

Fight, Flight, Freeze, Fawn Response A survival response that occurs in the body of an individual with a perceived threat designed to help protect the individual from pending danger.

Growth Mindset A belief that skills can be improved with effort.

Hippocampus This is the part of the brain that is responsible for memory and learning.

Hypervigilance This state that results in increased alertness for the potential danger that often occurs with individuals with a trauma history.

Hypothalamus This structure in the brain serves as a type of thermostat to help regulate various processes in the body. It is sometimes referred to as the master gland as it makes and releases various hormones in one's body.

Kazdin Method This method developed by Dr. Alan Kazdin is used to help parents learn how to respond to a defiant child.

Limbic System This is a group of structures in the brain (amygdala, thalamus, hypothalamus, hippocampus, insula, and a few other structures) that help to regulate emotions, memory, and behavior.

Magnetic Resonance Imaging (MRI) A medical procedure that collects images of soft tissues including the brain, muscles, and organs.

Maladaptive Behaviors These behaviors prevent individuals from adapting and adjusting. They prevent an individual from adapting to a new or difficult situation. They can include avoidance, self-harm, aggression, anger, defiance, etc.

Neuroception This is the ability of an individual to scan their environment for signs of danger and safety.

Neuroplasticity The ability that the brain can change and adapt over time.

Neuroscience The science that studies the structure and function of the brain and nervous system.

Neurosequential Model A model developed by Dr. Bruce Perry that integrates trauma-informed care practices with a neurobiological framework

Neurotransmitters Chemicals in the brain that send signals to various nerves, glands, and muscles in the body.

Noncontingent Escape (NCE) This is a behavioral strategy that provides an escape from a non-preferred task on a regular interval with the goal of reducing escape-maintained behaviors.

Noncontingent Reinforcement (NCR) This is a behavioral strategy that provides attention at regular intervals (independent of behavior). It is often used to help reduce behaviors that are maintained by attention. If a child acts out to gain attention, this procedure will involve providing regular attention to your child to reduce the probability they will engage in maladaptive behaviors to gain attention.

Post-Traumatic Stress Disorder (PTSD) A mental health condition that is caused by exposure to a trauma event that results in psychological impairment.

Prefrontal Lobe This is the part of the brain that is right behind your forehead. This part of the brain affects your personality, behavior, and thinking processes. When an individual is in a heightened state of fear, their prefrontal lobe is temporarily short-circuited so the quick, reactive limbic system of the brain can operate.

Premack Principle This behavioral strategy involves reinforcing a less preferred activity/behavior by a more preferred activity/behavior. For example, one can say, "eat your vegetables (less preferred), then you get dessert (more preferred)".

Pivotal Response Training (PRT) This is a behavioral training program that targets certain pivotal skills such as motivation and self-management. Providing choices is a key component of PRT.

Positive Emission Tomography Scans (PET) This is a medical scan that can provide images of the metabolic and biochemical functioning of various tissues and organs.

Posttraumatic Growth This is growth that can potentially occur after experiencing a traumatic event or situation.

Priming This is a way to help prepare your child about what is about to happen. Often, it involves sharing expectations.

Proactive Strategies These are strategies that a parent or caretaker does to try to prevent maladaptive behavior from occurring.

Responding Strategies These are strategies that a parent or caretaker does by responding to a child who is engaging in a maladaptive behavior.

Retribution Effect This effect sometimes occurs when a person who is being punished seeks to engage in additional behaviors to show disapproval or harm to the person who is providing punishment.

Teaching Strategies These are strategies that a parent or caretaker does to help teach new skills to a child to reduce maladaptive behaviors.

Thalamus The thalamus is a small structure in the brain that serves as a relay station for motor movement and sensory input.

Trauma-Informed Care (TIC) A philosophical approach to help health-care workers learn how to support their patients with a trauma history.

Trauma-Informed Parenting (TIP) A philosophical approach to help parents learn how to support a child with a trauma history.

Trauma-Informed Foster Parenting (TIFP) A coin termed by Dr. Adams to refer to how foster/adoptive parents incorporate principles of trauma-informed parenting (TIP) for how they interact and engage with the children in their care.

Trust-Based Behavioral Intervention (TBRI®) A model developed by Dr. David Cross and Dr. Karyn Purvis that helps parents learn how to empower, connect, and correct their children.

Index

For Product Safety Concerns and Information please contact our EU
representative GPSR@taylorandfrancis.com
Taylor & Francis Verlag GmbH, Kaufingerstraße 24, 80331 München, Germany

www.ingramcontent.com/pod-product-compliance
Lightning Source LLC
Chambersburg PA
CBHW052005270326
41929CB00015B/2794